GREEN URBAN
LIVING

GREEN URBAN LIVING

SIMPLE STEPS TO
GROWING FOOD · KEEPING CHICKENS
WORM FARMING · BEEKEEPING
AND MUCH MORE
IN NEW ZEALAND

JANET LUKE

NH
NEW
HOLLAND

First published in 2011 by New Holland Publishers (NZ) Ltd
Auckland • Sydney • London • Cape Town

www.newhollandpublishers.co.nz

218 Lake Road, Northcote, Auckland 0627, New Zealand
Unit 1, 66 Gibbes Street, Chatswood, NSW 2067, Australia
86–88 Edgware Road, London W2 2EA, United Kingdom
80 McKenzie Street, Cape Town 8001, South Africa

ISBN: 978 1 86966 322 3

Publishing manager: Christine Thomson
Editor: Sue Copsey
Book design and illustrations: Yasin Karadeniz
Cover design: Yasin Karadeniz
Back cover: from top to bottom; Chicken wrangling at dusk; Red spring onions; Burying an olla.

National Library of New Zealand Cataloguing-in-Publication Data

Luke, Janet.
Green urban living : simple steps to growing food, keeping chickens,
worm farming, beekeeping and much more in New Zealand / author,
Janet Luke ; design, Yasin Karadeniz.
Includes bibliographical references and index.
1. Gardening—New Zealand. 2. Sustainable living—
Handbooks, manuals, etc. I. Title.
635.0993—dc 22

10 9 8 7 6 5 4 3 2 1

Colour reproduction and printing by Craft Print International Ltd, Singapore.

CONTENTS

INTRODUCTION

WHEN I WAS YOUNG, I DREAMT OF LIVING ON A FARM AND BEING SURROUNDED BY ANIMALS. BUT THE REALITY IS THAT I DON'T WANT TO GIVE UP LIVING CLOSE TO FRIENDLY NEIGHBOURS, OR BEING ABLE TO WALK TO SHOPS AND SCHOOLS. IS IT POSSIBLE TO HAVE THE BEST OF BOTH WORLDS? I THINK IT IS. THANKFULLY I HAVE FOUND A WAY TO PRODUCE MUCH OF OUR OWN FRESH FOOD, KEEP SOME MICRO-LIVESTOCK, AND STILL HAVE A LIFE.

A plum tree needs a warm sunny position and will produce its first crop in around three years.

I've always enjoyed growing food, and, since having our three children, have become increasingly concerned about the state of our environment and the rising cost of living. I want my kids to know where food comes from and how to grow it. I also want my family to do its bit for the environment. And, as I have Scottish heritage, I want to save money and learn to live a more frugal lifestyle without having to give up my daily lattes! Being lazy, I also want to do this with the minimum effort.

We live in sunny Hawke's Bay, on the East Coast of New Zealand's North Island. We bought our house five years ago in the urban setting of Havelock North. Since then I have been ripping out roses and flowering shrubs, and planting fruit trees and other food-producing plants. I have created a low-maintenance garden that keeps my family, our neighbours and friends in produce most of the year.

As a mother of young children I don't have the time to be in the garden every day. My method of gardening is therefore based on sustainable principles that take out much of the hard work needed to sustain a conventional food garden.

Chickens are the best 'ecopets' kids can have. Baby chicks teach kids to be responsible and gentle.

It is organic and low cost, and uses the age-old concepts of companion planting, heirloom varieties of plants, and beneficial insects. As well as plants there's an assortment of poultry – my secret weapon when it comes to pest control and fertiliser. Along with three young sons, two worm farms, bees, a one-eyed frog, a dog, a cat, a rabbit – oh yes, and a husband – I have quite a menagerie. This way of living and gardening is all about making small, simple changes to the way you and your family live, so that you can save money, grow fresh food and reconnect with nature – and hopefully have fun doing so. With green urban living (I call this 'gurbing') there are no hard and fast rules or set ways: you can pick and choose the aspects that suit your lifestyle, your available commitment

Using recycled materials is one of the principles of green urban gardening. I often use empty toilet rolls as bio-degradable pots. Each is planted with a seedling, and breaks down quickly, avoiding disturbance to the roots.

and circumstances. You may choose to just have a worm farm on your apartment balcony, or perhaps grow some herbs in pots. You may want only to catch some rain in a rainwater barrel so you can wash your car with a clear conscience. Alternatively you may wish to fill your quarter-acre urban garden with vegetable beds, chickens, a beehive and a mini urban orchard. By taking small steps, as a community and as a country – and maybe even as a global village – we can all make a difference.This book will help you to develop a productive, low-maintenance, poison-free and attractive garden, without heavy digging, weeding or having to spend your hard-earned dollars in the process. Much of this knowledge has been around for centuries. Other ideas are newer and require

My green urban garden: space for a swingball, chooks, fruit trees and a vegetable garden.

a different way of looking at things. This way of gardening combines and creates relationships between animal life, plants, water, climate, soil and man-made structures in a way that lets nature do the majority of the work, leaving you more time to enjoy life. Green urban living is about attempting to break away from consumerism, creating a lifestyle that is more rewarding.

The principles involved can be applied to any space, from a small apartment balcony to a quarter-acre section. It could be a new garden, or an established garden requiring some simple modifications. You can even set aside an area of a larger garden for some green urban living ideas and still have that landscaped, designed, formal garden to impress.

When you are gardening you are always learning – green urban living is not about getting everything right every time. I'm always trying new things: planting corn earlier or later in the season; growing new varieties of plants;

My 'crop circle' garden keeps us in constant supply of fresh vegetables with a minimum of effort.

developing new structures. Sometimes they work, often they don't – but if it all turns pear-shaped you can just pull it out, rip it down and start again: gardening's all about trial and error. Be prepared for disasters and failures – when working with nature it's impossible to avoid storms, late frosts, or a squadron of butterflies descending on your cabbages. But rejoice in your gardening failures as this helps keep gardening fun. And such failures won't significantly hurt your purse – the principles are underpinned by low cost, minimum effort, and recycling.

New Zealanders have one of the world's largest ecological footprints, topped only by the United States and Australia. One of the major contributors to our 'big feet' is food production. The more we can grow and produce ourselves, using sustainable and organic methods, the more we can reduce our own family's footprint. (If you are interested in trying to calculate your own ecological footprint, visit www.myfootprint.org) Buy embracing a greener lifestyle you improve your health, your bank account, and, ultimately, your overall quality of life. And perhaps most importantly, you aim to leave behind a planet that is in a better state for future generations.

See how it's done

Throughout the book there are links to short informative videos I have made and uploaded to Youtube.

To start you off, visit www.youtube.com/watch?v=3Y6DCqJrD-Y for a quick tour around my green urban living garden in summer.

You can also visit the Green Community Forum at www.greenurbanliving.co.nz

Here you can ask advice and share knowledge with other like-minded 'gurbers'.

Chucks Winter
Pumpkin

CHAPTER ONE

WHAT IS GREEN URBAN LIVING?

AS BACKYARDS GET SMALLER AND OUR URBAN LIVES BUSIER, IT BECOMES MORE OF A CHALLENGE TO GROW SOME OF OUR OWN FOOD AND LIVE SUSTAINABLY. HOWEVER, WITH A BIT OF PLANNING AND INNOVATION IT CAN BE DONE. BY WORKING WITH MOTHER NATURE IT IS POSSIBLE TO CREATE A PRODUCTIVE GARDEN WITHOUT BEING A 'SLAVE TO THE SPADE' EVERY WEEKEND. IF YOU CAN LIVE WITHOUT TRIMMED EDGES AND BLEMISH-FREE VEGES, I CAN SHOW YOU HOW TO 'GROW YOUR OWN' IN A SUSTAINABLE GARDEN – AND HAVE A LIFE TOO.

WORKING WITH NATURE

Green urban living is loosely based on the theory of permaculture. The philosophy behind permaculture is one of working with, rather than against, nature. The term derives from two words: permanent and agriculture, and the idea was developed in Australia in the 1970s, by Bill Mollison and David Holgram. It involves 'the conscious design and maintenance of agriculturally productive ecosystems that have the diversity, stability and resilience of natural ecosystems. It is also about a harmonious relationship of landscape and people, providing their food, energy, shelter and other material and non-material needs in a sustainable way' (Mollinson, 1988).

Permaculture is about emulating nature in a way that derives multiple uses from one space. A permaculture design observes the natural forces at work in a garden space, and then looks at ways to harness them – not overcome them, as a conventional design might. For example, a conventional design may see a poorly drained, boggy area as something needing drainage, whereas a permaculture design will see that area's potential for an aquatic wildlife habitat and an area in which to grow watercress, wasabi or water chestnuts.

You don't have to create an entire permaculture system – you pick and choose any principle or aspect that suits you. In this way the system can fit in with our busy urban lives and small urban spaces. My garden has multiple uses, and reuses and recycles materials instead of buying in new materials or products. It is a way of gardening that is low cost, organic, low maintenance and not constrained by a strict set of rules or guidelines. Perfect for all of us who are time poor and keen to save a few dollars!

This small urban garden can accommodate three chickens, a beehive and a productive vegetable garden. What was once an underutilised front garden has become a productive urban space.

HOW A GREEN URBAN FOOD GARDEN MIMICS NATURE

Nature	A conventional fruit and vegetable garden	A green urban food garden
Maintains itself	High maintenance, often with non-renewable resources; contains many plants that need nurturing	Designed in a way that requires little maintenance
Soil is alive with microorganisms, fungi and earthworms	Soil is often inactive due to over-tilling and digging, and the use of inorganic fertilisers and pesticides	Adopts the no-dig system; soil is created on-site through the use of layering and composting, and provides a perfect habitat for soil microorganisms and worms
Highly diverse range of plants and organisms	Often a monoculture or contains only a few hybrid species	Lots of plants and organisms chosen to thrive in a garden's microclimate
A balanced level of pests and beneficial insects	Use of inorganic poisons to control large numbers of pests; destruction of beneficial insects due to pesticide use	A healthy balance of pests and beneficial insects
Relies on natural rainfall	High water use necessary to irrigate garden	Sustainable methods of water use including swales, mulching and rainwater collection barrels
Many layers and functions	Single layer; sole function is to grow food	Multilayered planting and multifunctional uses of spaces
No cost involved	High cost of materials and plants	Requires little financial outlay; can be expanded as time and resources allow
Natural ability to deal with changing seasonal patterns	Exposed to fluctuations in weather; many plants lost during times of drought or frosts	Ability to create cooler summer and warmer winter temperatures through the development of microclimates
A variety of different plant species growing harmoniously together	Straight, neat rows, each of one type of crop	Plants put in singularly in mixed groups to take advantage of companion planting theory and beneficial planting; this helps to disguise crops from pests

Green urban living brings a different, broader, and I think more exciting focus to growing food. There are no hard and fast rules – more a set of design principles to follow. These principles copy what happens in natural ecosystems, such as those in our ancient New Zealand podocarp forests, in which there are millions of elements: trees, shrubs, birds, mammals, insects, fungi and microorganisms. Each element within this ecosystem has many roles and supports a number of other elements. For example, a tall tree provides homes to other epiphyte plants, insects, birds and other creatures. Its fallen leaves turn to leaf mould and compost the forest floor, and provide food and habitat to other insects, fungi and new seedlings.

FITTING GREEN URBAN LIVING INTO A SMALL CITY SPACE

Many people think that edible gardens are only for rural properties, or for large properties on the fringe of urban centres. But it is very easy to design and manage a small townhouse garden under this self-sustaining system. The primary design considerations are:

- lack of space

- lack of natural vegetation cover, and

- lack of time due to our busy lifestyles.

Generally only areas 1 and 2 (see below) can be developed. But it is certainly possible to grow some vegetables, have a few dwarf fruit trees, perhaps keep some micro-livestock, and, of course, make your own compost.

GREEN URBAN LIVING: THE PRINCIPLES

CREATING EASILY ACCESSIBLE AREAS

The garden is divided into areas according to their proximity to the house. These areas directly relate to the number of times you visit the area on a daily basis. With all things being equal, try to match the site with the best use for that area.

- **Area 1** could have, for example, the clothesline, herb garden, barbecue and entertaining area, play area, sandpit, lettuce garden, shade house or cold frame for growing seedlings, rainwater tank and tool shed.

- **Area 2** is the area for the main vegetable garden, the fruit trees (maybe in pots or espaliered along a wall), the chicken coop, the worm farm and compost area. Hutches for rabbits and guinea pigs are also here.

- **Area 3** is for larger fruit trees (e.g. peach and nectarine), nut trees, shade trees, avocado, nitrogen-fixing trees or windbreak hedges, and ground covers such as pumpkins. If you have a beehive it could be situated in this area. If your property is really small, why not incorporate the council-owned street verge to plant fruit trees? If you want to do so, first of all check where your street services run, observe the location of overhead power lines, and, of course, check with your council.

- **Area 4** can contain a semi-wild area – a place to grow comfrey and nettles (in a sunken bucket to stop them spreading), and tall, non-invasive grasses to provide seed heads for birds or over-wintering habitat for beneficial insects. Cut them down in spring to provide carbon material for the compost. Herbs such as borage and fennel can be grown here to attract insects, and nectar-rich blossoms for bees.

TOP TIP

Use the council verge or lawn area to grow wild flowers or buckwheat plants to encourage important pollinators into your garden.

Many urban areas may only contain areas 1 and 2 – there may not be enough room for elements found in other areas, such as ducks, geese, orchards and ponds. However, you may want to create a small area 4 by planting some native trees or shrubs to encourage birds and animals to visit.

MULTIPLE USES FOR EVERYTHING

Try and have everything in your garden serving at least two functions. If you can make it three you're a legend! This makes the space significantly more useful and productive. For instance, if you grow sunflowers in the garden, they can:

- provide a living screen

- form a windbreak

- attract pollinators, namely bees, into the garden

- be cut and sold or used indoors

- be used as a support for runner beans to climb up

- provide food for poultry (the seedheads)

- provide seeds for husking, eating or sprouting

and finally, when the plant has flowered, the stalks can be cut and added to the compost as valuable carbon material.

A beehive can be successfully kept within a small urban garden. The key is to locate the hive so that the bees do not cause a nuisance to neighbours and passers-by. Locate the hive near a tall hedge or fence to force the bees high into the air.

Chickens are another great example of something that has multiple uses:

- they provide eggs, meat and feathers

- housed in a 'chicken tractor' (see page 142), they garden for you, eating all weeds, weed seeds and pests

- their manure is nitrogen rich and great for the garden

- they are docile eco-pets for children

- if they are housed in a permanent coop adjoining a glasshouse, their body heat can provide heating for the glasshouse over winter

- they can be employed to turn over composting material, accelerating the process

- they can be used to break in new ground for gardens

- they can be used in an orchard to eat fallen fruit and fertilise under the trees

- if Wandering Willy (Tradescantia) or oxalis weeds are a problem in your garden, the chickens will devour these if left on the area for several weeks.

LOCATION, LOCATION

Locate elements in the garden where their needs are met, and where they meet some of your needs. For example:

- Place fruiting trees inside a permanent chicken run – the chickens can eat any fallen and rotting fruit; this feeds them while keeping the place tidy. The tree canopy provides the chickens with shade, and with cover from hawks. In turn, the fruit trees are fed naturally by the chicken manure.

- The soapwort plant (*Saponaria officinalis*) is a hardy perennial that produces a cleansing chemical when the leaves are rubbed together. Plant this next to an outside tap and you have soap readily available when you need to wash your hands before coming in from gardening.

- Grow lavender or rose-scented geranium near the clothesline. Drape sheets and pillowcases over these bushes to dry. Their scent will be infused into your linen as it dries.

Naturally infuse your washing with the scent of sunshine and lavender.

REHASH, RECYCLE, REUSE, REINVENT, REVAMP

A green urban garden uses waste as a resource. For example:

- vegetable scraps, the dust from vacuum cleaner bags and ash from the fire can be given to the chooks to eat, or spread through the garden

- twigs and woody branches can be used as supports or to protect seedlings from the birds; *Muehlenbeckia astonii* makes a great protector – I call it 'nature's wire netting'

- tin cans with their tops and bases removed can be placed over seedlings to protect them from birds, slugs and snails.

- old wooden window frames or plastic fridge bins can be used as portable glasshouses.

WORKING WITH NATURE

By understanding how nature works, we can encourage nature to help us. All that is required is a bit of lateral thinking. For example, beneficial insects such as ladybirds, lacewings and hoverflies will happily devour copious quantities of aphids, whitefly and caterpillars. All you need to provide is:

- shelter – build a Bug Hilton in your garden (see page 170) or provide a winter habitat in your ornamental grass

- food in the form of particular plants

- a spray-free garden, and

- a shallow pond.

The bugs will do the rest.

'This little gardener went re-re-re, all the way around her garden.' Get your thinking cap on and find ways to recycle objects in your garden, e.g. old fridge bins make great cloches, as do recycled window frames.

By providing a safe habitat for beneficial insects you help create an ecologically balanced organic garden. This bughouse provides narrow tunnels, which ladybirds, hoverflies and lacewings prefer for reproduction and hibernation. They also create garden art with a purpose.

ENCOURAGING DIVERSITY

A wide variety of plants – annuals, perennials and trees – ensure a year-round, interesting, nutrient-dense and tasty harvest. Today we grow only a very small percentage of the seeds that our grandparents grew – mass marketing from multinational companies has seen to that. Join a local seed-savers' club, buy old heirloom varieties and save and swap seeds with friends, neighbours and family.

Try growing some unusual fruiting shrubs and trees. Try mulberries, pepinos, orangeberries, cranberries, cocktail kiwifruit, elderberries or white sapote. Make a conscious choice to plant old heirloom fruit trees. Not only are many of these trees more naturally resistant to pests and disease, but also their fruit often contain more nutrients than modern-bred fruit trees. For instance, the Monty's Surprise apple, a New Zealand heirloom apple, came out top in a recent study of antioxidant levels in apples.

Growing heirloom seeds allows us to preserve the past and save for the future.

LETTING CHAOS REIGN

Don't strive to plant in neat and tidy rows. Plant your crops haphazardly, using every available space. For tender crops, create microclimates under taller crops. Mix and mingle plant varieties to help disguise tasty crops from pests – many pests hunt by sight, so a beautifully laid-out row of cabbages is much easier to find than a single cabbage planted amongst a taller crop of corn. Allow weeds to grow as a living mulch and to provide food for chickens. Allow some of your vegetables to bolt to seed. This will encourage bees and other beneficial insects into your garden.

Mixing and mingling allows plants some disguise from pests and creates benefits from companion planting.

GUARDING AGAINST NATURAL THREATS

Create your own food insurance policies by assessing the risks of your site. It could be lack of water, late frosts or wind. It will be different for every garden.

Frost

If frost is a threat, design strategies to protect your plants. Think of frost as flowing water – this helps you envisage how frost will settle in your garden. The coldest places are behind hedges, in shallows and dips, and in the lowest parts of the garden. Build rock-filled gabions to create a heat sink, and grow your tender trees and plants around and over them. A microclimate that raises the ambient temperature by two- to- three degrees will protect your plants from frosts. Plant curved hedging to allow frost to flow around your frost-sensitive plants. Use river stones or water-filled wine bottles as garden edging to create a heat sink. The sun's energy will heat the water inside the bottles during the day; at night that heat is released into the surrounding soil and plants.

Put all those used wine bottles to good use as a heat sink around your tender plants. During the day the water inside the bottle will warm, releasing that heat into the soil at night.

Lack of water

If lack of water is your biggest threat, install a water barrel at every downpipe from your house. Mulch the garden beds thickly and install sustainable irrigation methods through your garden.

MULTI-LAYER PLANTING

In a green urban garden a fruit tree will be part of a multi-layered relationship, and the fruit tree will be a multi-grafted type, growing several varieties. Under the fruit tree, weed-suppressing ground covers such as nasturtium, clover or comfrey will be grown. Bulbs, and perennials such as globe artichoke or Jerusalem artichokes and herbs can be planted around the drip line of the tree. Close to the tree there may be edible shrubs like blueberry, Chilean guava, white or red currants or pepino, as well as small acacia or ice cream bean trees, grown for their nitrogen-fixing properties. Climbers, such as passion fruit or hops, can be grown through the fruit tree. Mushroom-inoculated logs can be grown in the shade, in the leaf litter. Such a multi-layered strategy provides the opportunity to grow a much higher number of species and yield of food from the same area. This is perfect for an urban garden where space is always at a premium.

> ### See how it's done
>
> Watch green urban gardener Deana explain how she has turned her front garden into a productive space with a beehive, chickens, vegetables, fruit trees and edible flowers.
> http://www.youtube.com/watch?v=Qj-6Id0R9EM

CHAPTER
TWO

CREATING A GREEN URBAN GARDEN

THE THOUGHT OF STARTING A GARDEN AND GROWING SOME OF YOUR OWN FOOD CAN BE INTIMIDATING, ESPECIALLY IF YOU HAVE NEVER DONE IT BEFORE, OR YOU DON'T HAVE MUCH GARDENING EXPERIENCE. BUT STARTING AND MAINTAINING YOUR URBAN GARDEN DOESN'T HAVE TO INVOLVE A LOT OF WORK, AS LONG AS YOU GET THE PLANNING STAGE RIGHT.

Chooks love being fed all the excess leaves from our homegrown vegetables. Their dome is made from recycled materials.

Don't start out as if you are going to feed the neighbourhood – the secret is to start small. Once one bed is established you can start on the next. A garden should be an enjoyable place to pass time; somewhere to escape to with a cup of tea or a glass of wine. Vegetable gardens are not just about growing food, but also about creating a beautiful natural space that is good to be in!

A green urban garden has a different aesthetic to a more traditional potager-type garden. To the untrained eye, it may appear messy and unruly, but when you become aware of the relationships and processes happening, this unruliness becomes a finely tuned and designed space. I admit that I initially struggled with the apparent chaos of my vegetable garden – it must have been the landscape architect in me needing a constrained and ordered space. But after a short time I could see how easy and low care this way of growing vegetables was, and knew that I would never return to the more conventional way of growing.

TOP TIP

To keep animals out of your vegetable garden, grow gooseberries as a low, thorny but edible hedge.

Developing a vegetable garden shouldn't cost you a fortune. Of course you can buy raised gardens and all the paraphernalia that goes with them, but my whole philosophy in regard to gardening is, why fork out your hard-earned cash on these things? It will take you years, if ever, to earn it back in fresh, homegrown vegetables. Instead, you can build a garden out of easily sourced or recycled materials, and make your own compost. All it takes is a little planning so that your garden is set up the right way from the start.

'SANDWICH' GARDENING

If you are anything like me, you want a beautiful and productive garden with the least amount of effort. Here is one way to achieve this – and if you can make a sandwich you can do this sort of gardening!

Sandwich gardening is a system of layering that creates a healthy and fertile garden that requires no digging and no weeding. It is an organic process that is neat and efficient, using materials found around your house or neighbourhood to create wonderful fertile soil.

All you need to build a sandwich garden is lots of newspaper and a variety of natural ingredients such as compost, grass clippings, leaves, sawdust, straw, seaweed, animal manure – or anything else organic you can lay your hands on.

Sandwich gardens particularly suit an urban garden, as you are creating new soil. In an urban area there are often issues of soil contamination. Many residential areas have a chequered past, with some sites having a history of horticulture or heavy industry that has led to a build-up of toxic chemicals in the soil. By building a garden on top of these soils you are not putting any potential food in contact with harmful chemicals.

WHY BUILD A SANDWICH GARDEN?

- The garden edge only needs to be raised around 10 cm to achieve all the benefits of a sandwich garden.

- These gardens improve the soil that is already there; in fact, a sandwich garden can be built directly over clay, rock or even concrete. In a small townhouse you may only have a paved area – you can build a sandwich garden directly onto this. However, if you build onto concrete there will obviously be no earthworms under your garden, so throw a handful of earthworms in to help mix all the organic matter.

- The garden can be raised to avoid constant bending, or for people in wheelchairs. Old apple bins work perfectly for the elderly or disabled, as they position the garden at waist height. You can often get old apple bins from orchards or vineyards; remove the timber base, place on level ground and start creating a garden.

- A sandwich garden improves drainage of water through the soil.

- A sandwich garden creates a better use of space, as plants such as herbs and cherry tomatoes can be trailed over the raised edges. This means you can get more food than from a similar-sized conventional garden.

- As you don't walk on the beds, the soil is not compacted and no digging is necessary. The theory behind a sandwich garden is that you are trying to mimic nature. In a forest or bush area, leaves and forest debris fall and create layers, which plant roots, soil microorganisms and earthworms blend and turn into rich humus. These microorganisms need air passing through the soil to help them break down this organic matter. Walking on soil compacts the layers, slowing this process.

- A sandwich garden gives the garden a clean and tidy look, with the added structure of the raised edge. Even in the dead of winter, when the garden may be bare, the structure of the beds gives some form to the garden. There are no hard and fast rules about what shape your sandwich garden should be. It can be square, round, rectanglular or even a zigzag.

- In spring, the soil in a sandwich garden warms up faster than in a conventional garden, so you can get an earlier harvest of your favourite crops, such as early corn or tomatoes. This is because the sides of the garden beds act as a 'heat sink', warming with the sun during the day and releasing that heat into the surrounding soil during the night.

- In a sandwich garden you create such good, fertile soil that you can plant more intensively and grow larger crops. You won't need to worry about following the spacing recommendations on the back of a seed packet again! By planting intensively you get more food for your space, and less uncovered soil means fewer opportunistic weeds.

- Sandwich gardens require less maintenance and weeding. And any weeds that do find a space are easily pulled from the loose friable soil.

- If you are renting, move often, or have a very limited space, you can create a portable sandwich garden – a raised garden complete with wheels. This can be moved around a patio area to follow the sun, or can be moved out of the way if you are entertaining.

- You can make your sandwich garden from recycled or found materials – organic homegrown veggies for free!

My garden beds are intensively planted. This stops weeds growing, and you get more food from your space.

TOP TIP

Use pine needles as a mulch on your garden paths. They help to deter pests such as slugs and snails.

Sunflowers growing in a mobile planter.

DISADVANTAGES OF A SANDWICH GARDEN

So the benefits of a sandwich garden are many. But what are the drawbacks?

- Sandwich gardens do take some time and effort to build. You could pay someone to build it, but that partly defeats the purpose. The trick is to collect all the ingredients you need to make the garden and then, one sunny weekend, invite your friends or family around for a barbecue. With a small team of willing, but perhaps unsuspecting, workers you could build three two-metre square gardens in ten minutes Throw them a sausage afterwards to thank them for their help!

- There can be costs involved if you buy new products and compost. However, it is possible to build your garden for a very small cost or even for free – this chapter will tell you how.

- Sandwich gardens do require a lot of water in hot weather, as they are naturally well drained – that lovely warm, friable soil is very thirsty. Mulching the surface and using sustainable irrigation helps address this problem.

Top tips for tools

- To avoid losing your tools in the garden, paint the wooden handles in bright colours.

- To keep garden tools clean, fill a bucket with sand and one litre of old engine oil. After using a garden tool dip it in and out of the sand mixture several times. The abrasive sand will clean and the oil will protect.

BUILDING A SANDWICH GARDEN: A STEP-BY-STEP GUIDE

Step 1: Decide what materials to use

Stones and rocks: most landscape suppliers stock river stones, or other local stone. Remember, it is illegal to collect river stones from the river. If you have a local quarry, they may sell rocks. Take a trailer!

Wood: old wooden apple bins or pallets can be reused as timber edging – hardware or timber merchants often have a pile of pallets they are keen to get rid of. Avoid using treated timber, but if you have no option, use weed matting as a liner between the soil and timber. Railway sleepers can be bought from most DIY stores. They are generally made of macrocarpa, and will eventually rot; you may only get five to eight years out of them. Recycled original railway sleepers, or sleepers made of eucalyptus or elm, are much more durable.

Naturally processed fertiliser: pony clubs or riding stables are a good place to source horse manure. If you have stockyards in your area, free manure is often available. Poultry farms and farmyard zoos also have an endless supply of manure. I often knock on doors and ask if I can collect the manure. People may think I'm crazy, but at least it's free.

Reused hard stuff:

- Check in the local newspaper classified ads – often people want pieces of broken concrete removed for free.

- Second-hand dealers, Salvation Army stores or auction houses will often have chipped plates, etc. to give away.

Other natural organic options

- **Autumn leaves:** ask at your local school or kindergarten if you can rake the leaves for them. Neighbours also often want somewhere to dispose of leaves. Try putting a sign at your gate saying 'autumn leaves drop-off' and see what happens.

- **Mulched organic matter:** aborists and landscapers can often drop off mulched organic matter for free. Bark mulch is best to use on paths; mulched leaves are great for the garden.

- **Food waste:** restaurants, school kitchens, rest homes, kindergartens, greengrocers and local supermarkets all have food waste which you may be able to collect. Take a large lidded bucket.

- **Flattened cardboard and paper:** recycling bins behind shops and factories are often full of this.

- **Pet hair:** pet groomers can supply bags of pet hair.

- **Straw bales:** building sites sometimes use straw bales for stormwater protection. Ask if you can have the bales when the building is completed.

- **Shredded paper:** offices may have quantities for collection.

- **Lawn clippings:** walk around your neighbourhood with your wheelbarrow on a fine weekend when people are mowing their lawns and ask for their lawn clippings (yes – I am that person!).

- **Untreated sawdust:** try asking a furniture maker or builder for their untreated sawdust.

- **Coffee grounds:** try asking your local café for used coffee grounds.

Step 2: Create an edge

Once you have selected the site for your vegetable garden, the area can be structured with an edging. This is not absolutely necessary, but it does retain the soil and keeps the garden looking neat. The edge can be only 10 cm high, or up to waist height if required. Materials that you can use to create an edge include:

- bricks
- river stones or limestone
- untreated timber
- discarded dinner plates sunk into soil on their edge
- railway sleepers
- large blocks of firewood
- lengths of old roofing iron
- old telephone books stacked four-high – they will eventually rot, but this will feed the soil carbon

Edging made from large blocks of firewood.

- concrete blocks

- recycled real estate signs cut to size and used as edging

- hay bales

- wine bottles, filled with water with caps on and placed into the soil necks down; the water warms up in the sun, acts as a heat sink and creates a microclimate (it also shows your neighbours what a wine lush you are!)

- 'urbanite' – broken pieces of concrete paths (about the size of a large dinner plate) stacked on top of each other

- large pieces of driftwood collected from the beach – an edge and garden art in one structure!

- large cardboard boxes – even these will provide support for a season.

Wine bottle edging is very effective – but not recommended if you have children who love fighting with sticks and throwing balls!

An edging made from locally sourced rocks.

Step 3: Lay newspaper or cardboard

If you are creating a garden over grass it is not necessary to spray weed killer over the area as the grass will die anyway – and remember, we want to grow organically. Put down layers (at least eight pages thick) of wet newspaper. Wet the paper with a hose as you go. Use normal newspaper: avoid glossy coloured paper as this contains harmful chemicals. Make sure the layers of newspaper are interlaced so that no soil is showing. Avoid doing this on a windy day to save your sanity. Cardboard, flattened boxes, old woollen blankets or natural fibre carpet can also be used.

This layer works as a natural weed matting to kill any grass or weeds. As they get wet, the fibres of the paper knit together creating a thick barrier. These wet layers are usually eaten by fungi, bacteria and worms within a few months – long enough for any weeds and grass to be killed.

Step 4: Create layers

The next step is to add layers of organic material to build up the garden to the required height. As you place each layer, wet it thoroughly with a hose as it needs water to function properly. (However, avoid getting it too wet and soggy.) Scatter a handful of blood and bone or animal manure over each layer. Keep layers about 10 cm thick, and, if possible alternate green matter with brown matter (see table below). Any type of organic matter can be used, but it is important to include grass clippings or animal manure as these are high in nitrogen and start the composting and breakdown of all these materials into soil.

Step 5: Final compost layer

A final layer of about 10 cm of weed-free, well-rotted compost provides an instant growing medium for your plants. (For information on composting, see Chapter 7.) If you want to save on compost, create small pockets where you want to plant seedlings, fill with compost and then plant into them. Alternatively you can let the garden sit for two months and let nature turn these newly constructed layers into rich compost. But if you are anything like me, you want to get plants in straight away and get growing your own food.

EXAMPLES OF ORGANIC MATERIAL TO USE IN A SANDWICH GARDEN

Green matter (nitrogen-rich)	Brown matter (carbon-rich)
Hedge clippings – cut into 10-cm pieces	Pea straw
Coffee grounds (brown coloured, but 'green' as they are nitrogen-rich) – collect from your local café	Lucerne hay or straw
Weeds from the garden – but avoid anything with seed heads or bulbs	Fallen leaves
Wool dags	Pine needles
Wilted comfrey leaves: make sure you let the cut comfrey leaves lie in the sun for a few hours to really wilt, otherwise you may get comfrey growing amongst your veggies	Human and pet hair (best to avoid chemically treated hair – like mine!)
Lawn clippings	Small twigs and sticks
Seaweed	Nut shells, e.g. pistachio and peanut shells
Animal manure	Shredded newspaper
Mushroom compost	Untreated sawdust (use sparingly)
Kitchen vegetable scraps	Feathers

Save money on compost and plant into pockets of compost on top of your sandwich garden.

See how it's done

Watch me demonstrate how to make a sandwich garden using easily sourced materials at:
www.youtube.com/watch?v=qbSsggpnpvE

TOP TIP

- If you don't plan to grow anything over the winter, cover your vegetable garden with a layer of sheep dags, an old woollen blanket or a piece of wool carpet. This will stop weeds growing and encourage earthworms up into the top layers of the bare soil.

- Bury some mothballs just below the soil surface – it deters cats from scratching the soil.

GROWING PLANTS FROM SEED

A punnet of six seedlings from the garden centre costs around the same as a packet of seeds, which will, depending on the type of plant, have over 100 seeds in it. Not difficult to work out which is more cost effective!

Growing plants from seed can become slightly addictive. Each season you want to try growing different varieties. This is when it makes good sense to swap or share seeds with neighbours and friends.

There is something very satisfying about raising vegetables from seeds. If you're really keen, seed raising will open up a huge world of hard-to-find heirloom varieties. These old-fashioned types are the ones our grandparents may have grown. Not only do they have great names, like Black Krim and Purple King, but they also have that great old-fashioned taste.

TOP TIP

Before gardening, scrape your fingernails along a cake of soap. This stops soil from lodging under nails and prevents them from chipping.

Recipe for seed-raising mix

- 1/3 coarse river sand (if you live near a West Coast beach you can use washed ironsand – being black, it helps warm the soil faster, which encourages seed germination)

- 1/3 compost

- 1/3 vermicasts from your worm farm

Mix well in a bucket and use as needed.

Reuse punnets from garden centres, or make your own out of takeaway coffee cups, yoghurt containers, cut milk bottle bases, wooden wine boxes, or ice-cream containers. Make sure you make drainage holes in the bottom of each container.

Seedlings being grown in paper pots and empty toilet rolls. Plant the paper pots straight into the garden to avoid disturbing the tender roots. The paper will quickly break down.

Many seeds can be sown directly into your vegetable garden, but I find I get a better germination rate if I raise seeds in containers and then plant them out when they are larger. If you have the time, make your own seed-raising mix (see recipe), or if not you can buy this from the garden centre.

Don't throw away all those empty containers. Reuse them as seedlings pots for your garden.

Wooden wine boxes make good seed-raising containers.

PLANTING SEEDS: A STEP-BY-STEP GUIDE

Step 1: Fill the seed-raising container

Fill your seed-raising container almost to the top with the seed-raising mixture, press down lightly and water.

Step 2: Plant your seeds

Plant your seeds: a general rule of thumb is to plant each seed as deep as it is large; for example, beans can be planted 2 cm deep, but lettuce seeds, which are really fine, are best scattered

TOP TIP

Top tips for seed-raising containers

Shared by Kayo, Green Community Forum

• Eggshells and egg cartons are both useful for raising seedlings. When you are breaking an egg, remember to do so carefully so that you have two neat halves in which to plant seeds. Once a seedling is ready for planting, put both the plant and its eggshell in the garden, so avoiding any root disturbance. The shell will rot quickly and provides nutrients to the growing seedling.

• Empty yoghurt pots make great seed-raising containers, particularly for cucumber, courgette and tomato plants.

• Make individual seed planters from empty toilet rolls or newspaper shaped around a small bottle. Many seedlings don't like root disturbance when they are planted out; these containers can be planted straight into the soil as they will soon break down.

TOP TIP

The secret to growing seedlings is to make small and successive plantings. It is very easy to be overenthusiastic and plant 50 tomato seeds resulting in 50 tomato plants all needing a home. When I remove some seedlings from the cold frame to harden off, this reminds me to sow a few more seeds. This way you have a small but constant supply of vegetables through the growing season – not one big glut early on.

Step 3: Label your seeds

Label your seeds – even if you think you will remember what they are, take the time to do so as it is easy to forget what you planted where. Make labels from old iceblock sticks or the lids from ice-cream cartons (see following Top Tip).

TOP TIP

Plant labels from ice-cream carton lids

Shared by Kate Brown, Green Community Forum

Cut the lid into strips – you can cut to the correct width to fit in the slots of reused garden centre pots. A permanent marker works well on the plastic – when you want to reuse the labels, simply wipe off using methylated spirits.

Step 4: Put your seeds in a suitable site

Find the best available spot for your seedlings. During the summer they will need some shade; in the cooler months put them in a cold frame, a mini glasshouse, or on a windowsill. Most seeds require a soil temperature of 15°C to germinate. Eggplants, tomatoes and capsicum require temperatures at a steady 20°C.

Step 5: Water your seeds

Water your seeds daily using a mist sprayer, not a hose, to prevent blasting the seeds out of their pot. Don't let the mixture dry out.

Step 6: Troubleshooting

If you find your seeds are not germinating well, this is most often because they have been planted too deeply or have not been kept constantly moist. However, if your seedlings suddenly keel over, wilt and die, this could be caused by 'damping off', a soil-dwelling fungal disease that affects seedlings. To help prevent this problem, for which there is no cure, avoid sowing the seeds too thickly, and try and maintain air movement around the seedling containers. I also use a chamomile tea solution to protect against it (see following Top Tip).

TOP TIP

Preventing damping off

Shared by Lou, Green Community Forum

• Take two chamomile tea bags and pour 250 ml of boiling water over them. Allow to steep for half an hour. Remove tea bags. When cooled, pour into sprayer bottle and use (undiluted) to water emerging seedlings for the first two weeks.

• Pre-soak seeds in a small amount of water containing two crushed garlic cloves. Garlic has an antifungal property so will help to naturally protect seedlings.

Step 7: Hardening off

When the seedlings have developed their adult-shaped leaves and are around 10 cm tall, they are ready to be planted out into the main garden. Place them in their containers next to the seed-raising area for several days to 'harden them off'. This process allows the delicate seedlings to acclimatise to the temperatures and conditions they will experience in the open garden.

Tomato seedlings hardening off prior to being planted in the garden.

Step 8: Planting out

Preventing damping off the best time to plant seedlings into the garden is in the cool of the evening or on a cloudy day. Avoid a scorching-hot day as the seedlings may get stressed and die. Try to avoid touching and disturbing the seedlings' roots – they are like delicate hairs and very fragile. For each seedling, make a small hole in the soil, place the seedling into the hole and gently firm the soil around the plant. Seedlings in paper pots or toilet rolls can be planted directly into the soil – the containers will rot down and the roots will not be disturbed. Just make sure all the cardboard or paper is below the soil line.

See how it's done

Watch six-year-old Edwin demonstrate how to. plant tender vegetable seedlings in the garden at:
www.youtube.com/watch?v=TfMbeODte88

Paper pot seedlings ready to be planted out in the garden. Choose a cloudy day or plant in the evening to avoid stressing the tender seedlings.

Step 9: Water and protect

Water the seedlings well for the next week while they are getting established. You may need to protect them from birds, slugs and snails. Try using tin cans with the bottoms cut out placed over the seedlings, or some 'nature's wire netting' (see page 19).

TOP TIP

Shared by Kate Brown, Green Community Forum

For cheap and effective cloches to help give seedlings a head start in the colder months, use clear plastic veggie bins from old fridges. In the summer they can be used as drawers in the garden shed. Look out for them in roadside inorganic collections.

Old fridge bins provide protection from the cold, and from garden pests such as birds and snails.

How to turn an old school desk into a cold frame

A cold frame creates the perfect warm microclimate in which to germinate seedlings, allowing you to start raising your seedlings while it's still too cold to do so in the garden. Here is a cheap and simple way to make your own seed-raising cold frame. You should be able to find an old school desk at a second-hand dealer or Salvation Army store, or by asking your friendly school caretaker for any broken ones.

Materials

- 1 school desk
- 1 sheet of clear perspex (from a hardware store)
- 4 screws
- chalkboard paint (a great optional extra: the black colour helps to warm the soil, and you can write directly onto the desk, in chalk, the date and varieties of seeds you have planted)

Tools

- handsaw or jigsaw
- screwdriver
- cordless drill

Method

- Unscrew the wooden lid from the desk (leave the hinges on the desk).
- Cut a piece of perspex to the same size as the lid, with a handsaw or jigsaw.
- Drill screw holes into the perspex, and affix the perspex to the desk using the hinges. (Some desks have a gap at the front that you can choose to cover with a strip of perspex as well.)

- Seal the desk with a paint sealer, and then paint.
- Place in warm sunny position under some shelter – next to the sunny side of the house, under the eaves is perfect.
- Prop open the clear lid on sunny days, and close when you tuck up your seedlings each night.

A cold frame made out of an old school desk.

HARVESTING AND COLLECTING SEEDS

If you collect seeds from your own plants you can truly become self-sufficient with your vegetable growing. Let a few plants of the type you want to grow again go to seed. You could choose a variety that you particularly enjoyed eating, or one that was pest-resistant or that grew with little watering or care. By choosing these sorts of plants you are breeding plants that are best suited to your environment and lifestyle.

Harvest seeds on a dry, sunny day – collect seedheads in a paper bag. Seeds can look very different from the parent plant so it is important to label them well.

Seeds come in a variety of natural packaging. It is a good idea to let the seeds dry completely on the plant, and then it is often a matter of simply shaking the seeds into a container.

A word of warning

Don't try saving seeds from any plant that is a hybrid, as they may develop differently to their parent. Hybrids or F1 plants have been crossbred for certain characteristics, but the seeds are often not true to the parents' characteristics and revert back to the original stock. Many seedlings that are bought from garden centres are hybrids. Look for the word 'hybrid' or 'F1' on the label when you are buying them.

Let the seeds dry out completely on the plant until the seeds or seedpods are brown and the pods are starting to split. If you shake the pod you should be able to hear the seeds rattling inside. Harvest seed on a hot, dry day, around midday, so that any morning dew has dried from the seeds. Beans and other large seeds are the easiest to collect. Small seeds may need to be shaken in a sieve. This helps to separate the seed from the husk.

Winnowing

Winnowing is a method used to separate the seed from the husk. Choose a day with a gentle breeze. Lay an old white sheet on the ground, and put a large bowl on it. Put your seeds into another bowl; raise them above your head and pour into the empty bowl. The breeze will help to separate the husks from the seeds – the seeds are heavier, so will fall into the bowl while the husks will be blown away.

STORING YOUR SEEDS

Place your collected seeds in the freezer for 48 hours. This will kill any stowaway insects that could eat the seeds when in storage. Then store the seeds in paper bags or envelopes, and label with the variety and date collected. Store in a cool, dark place. It is best to plant the seeds during the next growing season, as some varieties don't keep very long.

Harvesting seeds contained in a pulp

The seeds of tomatoes and cucumbers are contained inside a fleshy pulp. To save these sorts of seeds, choose the best fruit from the plant, cut open, and scrape out the pulp and seeds with a teaspoon. Place this pulp in a glass jar and half fill with tap water. Leave on a sunny windowsill for three days. During this time the pulp will start to ferment and a thick froth will collect at the top of the water. After three days the viable seeds will have sunk to the bottom of the jar. Drain and dry them on a paper towel. Store in a paper envelope for next season.

TOP TIP

Top tips for storing seeds

• Store seeds in a dry and cool place. Humidity and warmth will shorten their shelf life.

• As an alternative to paper bags, store seeds in 'snaplock' plastic bags, film canisters, medicine bottles, or glass jars with screw-top lids.

• To keep seeds dry, wrap three tablespoons of milk powder in some tissue paper and enclose with the seeds. Save silica gel packets from packaging for the same use.

• Dry seeds on paper towels and label by writing on the paper towel. When dry, simply roll up and put in a container. When you are ready to plant you can just tear off sections of the paper towel and plant seed and paper together in the soil.

• Use a large ring binder with plastic envelope sheets to store seed packets. They are then easy to catalogue and find.

• Always date the seeds. Most seeds only last three years, so you will know at a glance which ones need to be planted first.

Useful websites for seed lovers

New Zealand Seed Savers Network:
www.seedsavers.org.nz

Bristol Plants and Seeds:
www.bristol.co.nz

Kings Seeds:
www.kingsseeds.co.nz

Italian Seeds Pronto:
www.italianseedspronto.co.nz

Koanga Gardens (Centre for Sustainable Living):
www.koanga.co.nz

Ecoseeds:
www.ecoseeds.co.nz

Asian-seed:
www.asian-seed.co.nz

Egmont Seeds:
www.egmontseeds.co.nz

South Pacific Seeds:
www.spsnz.com

COMPANION PLANTING

One of the best things about companion planting is that it puts fun into gardening. There is something truly satisfying about outwitting a garden pest using only natural means. Some people may tell you that companion planting is just 'hocus pocus' – there may indeed be little documented scientific research to prove that it works. But I have found it to be effective; there is little cost involved, and at least you will be doing no environmental harm. It makes good sense to try and work with nature rather than trying to club it to death using chemicals.

Companion planting has been around for a very long time. There is evidence that the Romans practised it, and Native Americans developed 'The Three Sisters': pumpkins, beans and corn grown together.

The theory behind companion planting is that one plant will benefit another by either:

- hiding or shielding a crop from pests

- producing odours that confuse pests (e.g. onions planted next to carrots confuse the carrot fly)

- acting as a nurse plant, protecting a plant from wind, strong sun or frost (e.g. corn plants provide shade and cool conditions for coriander and lettuce planted underneath and around them, preventing these varieties from bolting to seed in the hot sun)

- secreting protective chemicals from their roots or leaves that deter pests (e.g. marigolds repel nematodes (soil-dwelling pests) from root crops such as carrots, parsnips and potatoes).

PLANTS TO PUT TOGETHER

Here are some examples of companion planting that work well in my garden.

- Plant foxgloves in and around your vegetable garden – it is believed they increase the vitality of plants nearby. They also attract bees and bumblebees (and look pretty).

- Plant a member of the onion family (e.g. garlic, spring onions, onions or leeks) next to carrots – the smell confuses pests.

- Plant marigolds with everything – if you only get round to planting one companion plant, make it this one. Be sure to choose the *Tagetes patula* species, as this one gives the most benefit.

Foxgloves are a biennial, which means they will flower the year after planting. They will self-seed if conditions are right.

Carrots planted next to garlic.

The Tagetes patula *marigold has the strongest smell, so it provides the most benefit. It will self-seed happily in the garden, but is not invasive.*

- Bubble and squeak: plant potatoes and peas together – they make great companions.

- Italiano: plant basil, tomatoes and parsley together.

(See Chapter 3 for more information on companion planting for vegetables.)

CROP ROTATION

Planting the same type of vegetable in the same place year after year causes a build-up of pests and diseases, and robs the soil of certain nutrients. The practice of crop rotation aims to avoid this. Put simply, change where you plant certain types of vegetables each year.

My style of planting does not generally have broad rows of one particular vegetable. I dot individual plants here and there, wherever there's room, making the best use of space and hopefully foiling the attacks from gangs of pests. However, I do attempt to follow a very simplified rotation plan. I remind myself where things were planted last season by making simple notes, often on the back of an envelope (which I normally abruptly lose). Follow this simple three-year system.

Divide your vegetables into three groups:

- **roots and bulbs** (e.g. carrots, potatoes, beets, leeks, onions)

- **fruits and seeds** (e.g. peas, beans, tomatoes, capsicum, sweet corn)

- **leaves and stems** (e.g. cabbage, cauliflower, broccoli, celery, lettuce).

Rotate these three types of crops so that each year they are grown in a new area of the garden, only returning to the original place in year four.

TOP TIP

Hang a cake of soap inside a mesh bag on an outside tap. To wash hands, just rub the mesh bag and rinse.

PEST CONTROL

Walk into any garden centre and you will find all manner of chemical warfare to take home to unleash on the creepy crawlies living in your garden. The trouble is, of course, that when we destroy the bad insects we inadvertently destroy the good ones. Furthermore, many pests become immune to the chemicals, and, in order to control these pests, we become trapped into using even more powerful systemic sprays. Pesticides and herbicides are harmful to the environment – to plant and animal life, and to nature's food chain.

Unlike conventional pesticides, homemade pest controls break down quickly. It can be argued that natural control methods are not as effective as more orthodox treatments, but with a little more time and effort they will control pests without harming your family or the environment, and will allow the good insects to thrive in your garden, helping to maintain a natural balance.

TOP TIP

To prevent caterpillars from crawling up the stems of garden plants, wrap sticky tape around the stems, sticky side out.

MAKE YOUR OWN PEST SPRAY

The following sprays will repel, and in many cases kill, pests, but remember that they are all contact sprays so need to be applied regularly, especially after rain, to be effective. All parts of the plant, especially under the leaves, need to be covered with the spray.

Any spray can be harmful, so when making them don't use everyday cooking pots, don't inhale fumes, ventilate the room, and wear gloves. Label all jars and store in a cool, dark, safe place. The shelf life of homemade sprays is limited and they are most effective when used fresh. Don't expect pests to drop like flies with these sprays – often it can take a few days, and reapplications are often necessary.

Rhubarb spray

Use against mildew and aphids, and any other sucking or biting pest. Rhubarb leaves are very poisonous so take care with its preparation, use and storage. Boil 1 kg of leaves in about 2 litres of water for 30 minutes. When cold, strain, and add enough soap flakes to make the mixture frothy. To use, dilute the spray by 50 per cent with water.

TOP TIP

Here is a great way to use every last bit of the rhubarb. Cut the stalk into segments and stew with sugar added for taste. Have in pies, crumbles or added to muffins. Drain the liquid and add some more sugar to this liquid to taste. This makes a lovely refreshing cordial when diluted with water or lemonade. The remaining leaves can be used to make the rhubarb spray.

Salsa spray

I use this spray on any plant that looks like it is being eaten. It is a real witch's brew, both in looks and smell, so open the windows when you are making it! Boil about 10 cloves of garlic, 5 red chillies and 2 chopped onions for about 30 minutes. Let stand overnight. Add a squirt of washing-up liquid to help it cling to the plant leaves. Store in a glass bottle. Mix one small cup of mixture to about 2 litres of water and use immediately.

Marigold spray

This kills most sapsuckers such as whitefly, scale and aphids. Fill a container with marigold flowers, cover with boiling water and leave to stand overnight. Strain and spray.

Pyrethrum spray

This kills all sucking and biting pests. Fill a container with pyrethrum flowers, cover with boiling water and leave to stand overnight. Strain and spray. This spray is toxic to bees, so only spray in the evening when the bees are in bed.

Bug juice spray

This one is especially good for green vegetable beetles and macabre gardeners. Apparently the smell of dead relations gets rid of the survivors. Collect and kill around 10–15 of the offending bugs. Put in a blender with 2 cups of water and whizz until homogenised! If you'd rather not use your cocktail blender you can use a pestle and mortar. This extract can be diluted. Freeze leftovers for using after rain. Add liquid soap before spraying onto plants. I have to admit I have only used this recipe once (I was banned from using the food processor), but it does work.

Baking soda spray

Use against powdery mildew and black spot. Mix 1 litre of water with 1 tablespoon of baking soda and 1 teaspoon of cooking oil. Add a squirt of soap flakes or washing-up liquid.

PEST TRAPS

Snail and slug traps

Make a trap using a glass jar pushed into the soil on an angle, half-filled with beer. The snail or slug will crawl in and drown. Or try making bait by mixing 1 cup of rolled oats or bran with 1 cup of borax and 1 cup of grated raw potato or kumara, then add maple syrup or golden syrup to make the mixture sticky. I put this bait under an upturned ice-cream container with a section cut out to form an entranceway. Snails and slugs will die after eating the mixture.

Snails are partial to a tipple of beer.

Make a 'shocking barrier' by placing copper tape around pots, or copper flashing around raised vegetable beds. The copper creates an electric fence for slugs and snails – they receive an electric shock if they touch the copper.

Pay children to collect snails! On a wet night I give each of my boys a torch and a container and place a 10-cent bounty on the heads of any snails caught. We feed the snails to the chooks as a treat.

Chooks love escargot sans garlic butter.

Clay masque

This will deal to any chewing or sucking insect and is especially good for aphids. You may need to reapply over several days. Mix 5 tablespoons of clay with 1 litre of water that has been boiled with 5 soap nuts for 10 minutes. Soap nuts can be bought in most health-food shops. They are a tropical fruit containing saponin, a natural cleansing agent. I use them to wash our clothes. The soap nuts add a natural stickiness to the clay mixture. Spray on any sucking or chewing insects – it suffocates the blighters.

Whitefly traps

Smother a yellow piece of cardboard in Vaseline or cooking oil spray, attach a string, and hang in a tree where whitefly are present. The whiteflies are attracted to the colour yellow and will get stuck in the oil. Clean and recharge the card with oil when full.

It is possible to do without chemical pest control, but the trade-off is some pests in the garden and maybe some damage to your crops. If it doesn't seem to work at first, remind yourself that nature is all about balance and it does take several years for a new organic garden to achieve that balance.

Sticky yellow card makes a great natural whitefly trap.

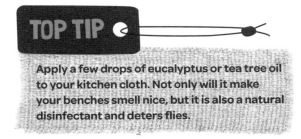

TOP TIP

Apply a few drops of eucalyptus or tea tree oil to your kitchen cloth. Not only will it make your benches smell nice, but it is also a natural disinfectant and deters flies.

Diatomaceous earth

Diatomaceous earth is a naturally occurring product formed from the fossil remains of algae. Each tiny grain is very hard and razor sharp. When diatomaceous earth comes in contact with insects, the razor-sharp edges lacerate the exoskeleton and the powder absorbs the body fluids, causing death from dehydration.

Organic health shops often stock diatomaceous earth in the gardening section. It is totally organic and natural with no toxic build-up or risk of pest tolerance. It looks and feels like very fine corn flour. I use it with great success in my garden – it has become my first arsenal of attack. The dust is easily washed off when you pick your vegetables.

Outdoor insects affected by diatomaceous earth include: ants, caterpillars, cut worms, fleas, ticks, cockroaches, snails, slugs, spiders, silverfish, lice, mites, flies, centipedes, earwigs, aphids, beetles, fruit flies, lemon tree, borers, thrips and psyllid. Diatomaceous earth does not harm earthworms.

There are two forms of diatomaceous earth: agricultural grade and pool grade. They are processed in different ways. Never use pool grade diatomaceous earth on your garden or animals.

Where to use diatomaceous earth

- Sprinkle on and around your vegetables to kill all sucking, chewing and rasping pests.

- Sprinkle a border of diatomaceous earth around tender seedlings to protect from snails and slugs.

- Dust around the chicken coop, kennels and sheds to kill lice, adult fleas and mites.

- Sprinkle on manure to kill flies and destroy odour.

- Apply a cup to compost piles to prevent pests and odours.

- Dust the undersides of leaves to target the tomato psyllid.

- Sprinkle around the base of house piles, foundations and wood stacks to keep away cockroaches and white-tailed spiders.

- Sprinkle at the bottom of rubbish bins and wheelie bins to kill ants.

- Mix 2 cups of diatomaceous earth with 500 ml of water, and paint around the base of wheelie bins, letterboxes and worm farms – or anywhere else where ants are a problem.

- Paint this solution onto the trunks of fruit trees to protect from ground-dwelling insects such as hatching codling moths.

- Sprinkle on windowsills to kill flies.

- Sprinkle under fridge, barbecue and oven.

- Apply to kitty litter to deodorise and absorb moisture.

How to apply diatomaceous earth

The most efficient way to apply diatomaceous earth is probably with a dust puffer. This makes it easy to treat hard-to-reach corners and cracks. Five hundred grams of diatomaceous earth will last a season, as the duster delivers a fine powder exactly where you want it. Alternatively you can use a flour sieve or a cheese shaker – but this does waste a lot of powder. Remember to reapply after rain.

I spray my vegetables in the morning when dew is still present. This helps the fine dust stick to the leaves. Alternatively you can wet the plants with a mist sprayer prior to applying the diatomaceous earth.

See how it's done

Watch me explain the uses and application of diatomaceous earth at:

http://www.youtube.com/watch?v=JKaAt4KxJyw
South Pacific Seeds:
www.spsnz.com

Please remember

Diatomaceous earth is a great product, but it is not clever enough to distinguish between pests and beneficial insects. Ladybirds, honeybees, hoverflies and lacewings will also be killed if they come in contact with the powder, so apply it only to areas where there is visual evidence of pests.
Avoid breathing the dust as it can irritate mucous membranes.

USING PLANTS TO CONTROL PESTS

Managing pests in your garden using natural control methods is nothing new. This type of control has been around for hundreds of years, as opposed to inorganic pesticides, which are relatively new on the scene. Biological control is best explained as attracting beneficial insects into your garden to suppress nuisance insects. Encouraging these good guys helps to maintain a healthy balance of insects and avoids the use of insecticides.

The good guys

- **Lacewings:** adult lacewings are often green and have wings similar to dragonflies', but they fold them to the sides. While the adults feed on pollen and honeydew, lacewing larvae are rampant eaters of thrip, scale, mealy bugs, mites and aphids. They do this so effectively that they are bred commercially and released into greenhouses to work their organic magic.

- **Praying mantis:** both the larvae and adults run riot with pests. One praying mantis can eat up to 20 flies each day. Their presence in your garden shows that you are achieving a balanced ecosystem.

- **Ladybirds:** these cute and iconic insects are ferocious hunters of aphids, mealy bugs, mites, the dreaded psyllids, whitefly and scale. In other words you can't ever have enough of them. Their most important role is in keeping aphids under control – an adult ladybird eats around 400 aphids before it is mature enough to breed. The most common ladybirds are red with black spots, but there are also yellow and steely blue species.

- **Hoverflies:** these look like miniature bees or wasps, but they move like a helicopter, darting this way and that. They eat nectar and pollen from plants such as fennel, dill, carrot and coriander. The larvae spend their waking hours sucking the innards out of aphids and juicy caterpillars.

- **Ground beetles:** beetles have Rottweiler-like jaws, and feed, usually at night, on caterpillars, slugs, ants, nematodes and snail eggs. They will even have a go at a passing grasshopper.

- **Earwigs:** most species of earwig recycle decaying organic matter and munch on smaller insects. They have an appetite for aphids, and are even more efficient at keeping their numbers down than lacewings and ladybirds. One species does have an appetite for flowers and enjoys nibbling on roses.

- **Bees:** these girls are really important for the pollination of flowers. Without them most of our food plants, like fruit trees, pumpkins and beans, would not set fruit. To attract them into your garden let some of your brassicas go to flower – they will seek out the nectar.

- **Parasitic wasps:** these guys look like a stripy, anorexic wasp with long dangly legs. These wasps lay their eggs inside a live pest, the eggs hatch and slowly eat their way out of the host. What a way to go!

- **Spiders:** these are probably the most important garden predators, even though they have an image problem with many people! They will eat flies, mosquitoes, caterpillars, codling moth larvae, butterflies and whitefly.

- **Native lizards:** our native lizards will eat slugs and snails, flies and many other insects. They will take up residence in your garden and make it their home for life if you provide some attractive real estate. Build a lizard lounge by layering some corrugated iron and small stones, and placing in a sunny spot.

- **Centipedes:** one of their favourite meals is slugs, with snail for dessert.

TOP TIP

If ants dine in your pet's food bowl, partly fill a shallow dish with water and put the food bowl in the centre of it, creating a moat. The ants can't swim across the water.

The bad guys

- **Aphids:** these guys suck the sap out of plants – you can often see them gathered at the top of the tender growing tips in large numbers. Flush them off with a short jet of water from the garden hose.

- **Mites:** these cause silvering of leaves and often make mini webs on the underside of the affected leaves. They are sapsuckers, robbing the plant of important nutrients.

- **Whitefly:** these are a close cousin of the aphids. They can build up to huge numbers in the warmer months. Brush past many brassicas, especially cavolo nero or citrus plants, and a white cloud of them will fly out.

- **Scale:** these immobile little turtle-like creatures suck sap from host plants.

- **Green beetles:** also known as stink bugs, shield bugs and green vegetable bugs, these pests will chew holes in your vegetables while their babies are busy snacking on the same plant's roots. Squash one and you will quickly find out why they are known as stink bugs. This characteristic smell is to warn other beetles that danger is about.

TOP TIP

Plant a cleome (spider plant) in the vegetable garden. This plant attracts the green beetles. You can then pick them off (and feed them to the chickens, if you have them).

Squash one of these and you will immediately discover why they are called stink bugs!

- **Carrot fly:** these like to bite deep holes in your prized carrots.

TOP TIP

Plant any of the onion family to help disguise the scent of carrots to these marauders (see page 39). You can also mulch around carrots with used coffee grounds – the smell helps to disguise the carrots.

- **Caterpillars**: the larvae of butterflies and moth.

Pests in my garden receive a double whammy with cleome and marigold plants.

TOP TIP

The best way to get rid of caterpillars is to pick them off. Attract birds into your garden to do the same job: try placing a birdbath or feeding station in your garden. You can also buy a certified organic treatment at your local garden centre. This spray contains a bacteria called *Bacillus thuringiensis* (Bt). It is the mainstay of all organic orchardists for the control of caterpillars. Just spray it on all leaf surfaces. Birds can eat the Bt-affected caterpillars without being harmed.

- **Mealy bug:** if you spot what appears to be cotton wool on your plants, you are the proud owner of thousands of mealy bugs. (Ladybirds and parasitic wasps will dispatch them, as will spraying oil, which suffocates them.)

- **Thrip:** these use their teeth to rasp the underside of leaves, resulting in a silvering of the affected leaves. They prefer camellias, azaleas and rhododendrons to food plants, but if you are growing a tea plant watch carefully, as it is from the same family as camellia. (Organic pyrethrum will treat mealy bug.)

TOP TIP

Cockroach poison

Mix equal parts of boric acid with flour or sugar. Sprinkle this mixture around sinks, fridges, the garage, woodstack, oven and under the dishwasher. When the cockroaches walk through the powder they groom themselves and are poisoned. Buy boric acid from chemists. Keep out of reach of children and pets. Large amounts can be toxic.

How to attract the good guys

The secret to getting the good guys to visit and stay for the duration of the growing season is to provide beneficial flowers from spring to late summer. This will involve planting every month to provide a continuous source of nectar or pollen.

Flowers with small, open flowers tend to be more attractive, as most of the beneficial insects have short tongues! Also, any umbrella-shaped flower will be attractive.

Here is a list of some easy-to-grow perennials and vegetables to tempt the good guys into your garden. Try growing them in and around your vegetable garden. Not only will they help protect your crops, but they also look pretty too.

- Phacelia: this is the equivalent of chocolate ice cream for the good guys. They will sniff this one out from far and wide. If you only have time to plant one attracter, plant this one.

- Carrot flower (collect seeds when flower dries)

- Coriander

- Parsley

- Queen Anne's Lace

- Fennel

- Cosmos

- Marigold

- Lupin

- Alyssum

- Echinacea (coneflower)

- Rudbeckia

- Native New Zealand plants that attract the good guys include muehlenbeckia, pittosporum, ribbonwoods, cabbage trees and hebes.

TOP TIP

To keep slugs and snails away, smear Vaseline under the rim of a pot with a flared lip, then sprinkle salt over the Vaseline. The salt does not get washed away as the lip protects it from the rain. This forms a simple but effective barrier for around six months.

All the good guys love Phacelia, especially bees and hoverflies.

Let some of your coriander flower to attract beneficial insects into the garden. Later you can collect the seeds to re-sow or for use in cooking.

A bumblebee filling up on parsley pollen. When parsley is flowering it forms a giant floating pillow, making it easy for the good guys to land on.

Fennel flowers look striking in the garden. Their big dinner-plate flowers make an easy landing pad for insects.

A monarch butterfly visiting a cosmos flower.

Plant marigold flowers with everything!

In winter, try to provide refuges such as long grass or hedges so the good guys will stay. You can make an insect home by putting bamboo canes inside a can, or for a great project with the kids build a Bug Hilton (see page 170) out of recycled materials and place it close to the vegetable garden. Beneficial insects will hopefully use this structure to hibernate in over winter and breed in during spring and summer – and you get some garden art to look at!

Leave a pile of logs or leaves in your garden to attract insect- and slug-eating hedgehogs.

Remember in an organic garden you are working towards an 'ecological balance'. To achieve this you need some pests to provide food for the good guys. Don't be too concerned if you have a healthy supply of aphids or caterpillars on some plants as this is all part of the natural cycle. You can always tell people you are breeding aphids to feed the pet ladybirds!

Where to buy extra good guys

Beneficial insects and bumblebees can be sourced at:
www.zonda.net.nz

USING RECYCLED MATERIALS IN THE GARDEN

Green urban gardens are all about reusing and recycling. I love fossicking around second-hand stores and auction houses, and even recycling bins, looking for materials to reuse in the garden. I love saving money (did I mention I have Scottish heritage?), and in this age of consumerism, where things are thrown away without hesitation, why not instead try to get into the habit of reusing or revamping, giving things a second life in your garden? The following ideas will hopefully get you looking at throwaway items in a different way and may even get you bottom up, head down in a dumpster!

Tender capsicum plants are kept warm and safe within their own private glasshouses. The stick through the top anchors the bottle when windy. As the plant grows and the weather warms, they are removed, stored and used again.

MINI GREENHOUSES

Use fizzy drink bottles as mini greenhouses. They provide a warm, moist environment protected from wind, frost and birds, and will get your tender summer crops, such as peppers, eggplants and tomatoes, off to a flying start. Cut the bottoms off the bottles and remove the screw tops. Secure with a thin stake through the neck of the bottle.

See how it's done

To see examples of the recycled glass houses and cloches I use in my garden, visit www.youtube.com/watch?v=XVNEH7uzIHU

TIN CAN PLANT PROTECTORS

Save all those baked bean cans and cut off the bases with a can opener. Use as plant protectors from those marauding birds and snails. Plant peas and beans inside the cans so the birds can't dig them out and eat them. They also create a barrier against slugs and snails. Takeaway coffee cups can be used in a similar way.

VENETIAN BLIND PLANT MARKERS

Don't throw out those old wooden or plastic venetian blinds – they make great plant labels. Cut into lengths with a hand saw or wire cutters and use to keep track of what is growing in your garden. You can use a piece of fine sandpaper to rub out old writing for next season. You can also make tree labels out of them. Drill a small hole in one end and thread with wire. Write the variety, rootstock and year planted on the label in permanent marker or paint. Attach the wire loosely to the tree.

PAUA SHELL BIRD SCARER

This is a fun project to do with the kids. Thread paua shells onto long lengths of fishing line, and hang them from bamboo stakes so they swing freely in the breeze. Position them over young plants to keep the birds away. You can do the same with old CDs.

WOOL DAG MULCH

If you know a sheep farmer or lifestyle block owner, collect crutching wool from them. Crutching wool comes from the back end of a sheep and is normally full of all that lovely organic stuff that makes your garden grow! Place this wool around fruit trees, under trees and shrubs at the time of planting, and around your vegetable plants. The wool stops weeds growing and retains moisture. When it rains any sheep manure is washed into the soil. The wool breaks down very slowly feeding nitrogen to the soil. Many people have told me that this type of mulch also deters possums. When it has been raining your whole garden smells like a wet blanket – not an offensive smell, but interesting nevertheless.

Dag wool seed mats

After seeing the many benefits of dag wool, I have been involved in creating a new product (called Woolgro Veggie Mats). These are thin mats of carded dag wool with a variety of vegetable seeds embedded inside. You roll them out on your garden, cover them with a thin layer of sand or compost, and keep them watered. The seeds are kept warm and moist, are protected from birds and heavy rain, and the wool mat acts as a weed mat. As the plants grow the wool and natural fertiliser feed the plants and the soil. After three months the wool has completely broken down, conditioning the soil.

COFFEE IN YOUR GROUNDS

Count the number of cafés in your neighbourhood and then think about the amount of used coffee grounds going to landfill. Approach your local and ask if you can collect their used coffee – most will be delighted to have it taken off their hands.

I collect two sackfuls a week from my local café and easily put it to good use inside and outside my home.

- **In the garden:** coffee grounds are high in nitrogen so are great to use in the garden. However, they are acidic, with a pH of around 6, so if you do use a lot of them in the garden apply garden lime at regular intervals to keep your soils pH neutral.

- **Mulch:** spread coffee grounds as mulch – smells great when it's raining. Firstly mix with leaves or grass clippings; this prevents the grounds from forming a hard layer over the soil. Spread thickly on paths to stop weeds growing.

- **Liquid fertiliser:** add coffee grounds to a water barrel with comfrey to make a great liquid fertiliser.

- **Snail defence:** to deter slugs and snails, mulch coffee grounds around lettuce seedlings and other plants that they find yummy.

- **Natural pest control:** lay coffee grounds as a thick border around your vegetable garden to deter insect pests.

- **Carrot protection:** when sowing carrots (and other tiny seeds), mix them with coffee grounds. This will deter the carrot fly pest, and ensure you don't plant seed too thickly.

- **Ant control:** instead of poison, sprinkle coffee grounds around the exterior of your house to deter ants.

- **Worm farm additive:** add coffee grounds to your worm farm; the worms will enjoy their caffeine kick.

- **Natural stain:** next time you need to stain a fence brown, try soaking coffee grounds in water for five days. Strain, and use the fluid as a low-toxicity fence stain.

- **Rodent deterrent:** putting coffee grounds in your compost is said to deter rats and mice. Apparently they are not big coffee drinkers.

TASTY TURRETS

Use recycled PVC plumber's piping to grow a vertical garden. The larger-diameter drainage pipes are ideal – you may be able to find them at your local demolition yard. Cut into lengths and then drill 3 cm-diameter holes in them (for planting in) using a hole saw. Hammer two bamboo or metal stakes into the ground and then slide the length of pipe over these. Fill with good-quality potting mix mixed with water-absorbing crystals and compost, and plant with strawberries, lettuce, spinach or herbs. Water from the top regularly. Your crops are protected from soil-dwelling insects, and, in the case of strawberries, it is very easy to net to protect from birds.

BIKE WHEEL CLIMBING FRAME

Old wheel rims are easy to find at bike shops. You can use them to construct climbing frames for beans and peas, with long lengths of bamboo and garden twine attached to ground pegs. Mature plants can be very heavy, so ensure your structure is strong.

Most bike shops will happily give away old wheels. I use them to grow my scarlet runner beans. Run bamboo stakes or twine from the wheel hub down to the ground and secure. Garden art with a purpose.

CHAPTER THREE

GROWING VEGETABLES

IN CHAPTER 2 WE DISCUSSED HOW TO CREATE AND MAINTAIN A 'SANDWICH GARDEN'. FOR GROWING VEGETABLES, ROUND–SHAPED SANDWICH BEDS GIVE YOU THE LARGEST AREA, AND YOU CAN PLANT HERBS OR PERENNIALS BETWEEN THE CIRCLES. IF YOU HAVE LIMITED SPACE, GROW VEGETABLES IN WINDOW BOXES, POTS OR HANGING BASKETS. CONSTRUCT SHELVES INSIDE A SUNNY WINDOW FRAME TO GROW DWARF TOMATOES AND POTTED HERBS. BUILD VERTICAL PLANTERS OR LADDERS TO MAKE THE BEST USE OF VERTICAL SPACE.

Growing vertically overcomes the challenge of limited space. This wooden planter lets you grow a good quantity of vegetables on a small patio or balcony.

WHERE TO LOCATE YOUR VEGETABLE GARDEN

- Most vegetables require at least six hours of sunlight every day during their growing season, so a north-facing site is ideal.

- If your garden is on a slope, create terraces for a more usable space.

- Overhanging trees create shade, so avoid these areas, or trim the trees. Remember that any deciduous trees you are looking at in winter will be in leaf in summer.

- Your vegetable garden needs to be near a tap for irrigation.

- Locate your vegetables relatively near to the house – you don't want to be trudging down to the end of the garden in the middle of preparing dinner.

- Soil conditions are not important, as the garden can be built up to provide new fertile conditions. This is especially handy in urban areas where soils are often infertile and compacted, or if an area has a history of industrial use, which may have caused a build-up of toxins in the soil.

- Vegetables need to be protected from the wind to do well. You could plant an edible hedge of feijoa or hazelnuts, plant rows of corn, artichokes or sunflowers, or use wind-screening material such as lattice.

- Start small – make the garden only as large as you can cope with (you can always expand it later). To grow all your vegetables and grain for a family you would need around 100 square metres! However, a three-metre square garden will be more productive, if done well, than a large one that gets away on you.

- To avoid walking on the garden beds and compacting the soil, make the beds narrow so that crops can be easily accessed from the edge. One metre wide by two metres long is a good ratio to start with.

TOP VEGETABLES TO GROW

POTATOES

Potatoes have become one of the world's most important crops, and, as the world price of rice continues to rise, they are likely to remain so. Unfortunately, because they grow underground, commercially potatoes are also the most pesticide-contaminated vegetable. Hazardous chemicals that have long been banned, but which linger in the soil, are found in commercially grown potatoes – to such an extent that the Environmental Working Group (a US not-for-profit environmental research organisation) warns parents not to feed them to infants and toddlers unless they are thoroughly washed, peeled and boiled. This makes an extremely strong case for growing them organically at home.

Always buy seed potatoes, as these will produce healthy, disease-free crops. Sprout them in a warm, light area. (I place the seed potatoes in an egg

If you grow your own potatoes you'll know exactly what sort of soil they have been grown in.

Sprout your seed potatoes in a warm sunny spot. An egg carton works well as a container.

carton and put them in a sunny corner.) Plant the potatoes when the sprouts are at least 10 cm long. To get a bigger crop you can cut the seed potatoes in half between sprouts. Plant in trenches about 20 cm apart, and cover with 20 cm of soil.

Wilted comfrey leaves laid on the bottom of the trench prior to planting will give a boost of nitrogen when the potatoes need it most. (If you do use comfrey leaves, make sure they are properly wilted, otherwise you will have a crop of comfrey with your spuds! I cut comfrey leaves on sunny days and lay them out on concrete for about three hours.)

Potatoes grow by developing more tubers up the root structure. This is why it is important to mound soil around the plant as it grows above the soil. Mounding encourages a bigger crop and prevents light reaching the tubers, which renders them poisonous. Mound up soil every couple of weeks when the plant is 20 cm above the soil level. Do this at least three times.

Wrap wilted comfrey leaves around seed potatoes to give each its own little growth booster.

Planting potatoes along a dug trench makes it easy to mound up the soil as the plants grow. This ensures you get a bumper crop.

TOP TIP

Shared by Woody, Green Community Forum

Instead of throwing rhubarb leaves (which are poisonous) in the compost, use them as mulch around your vegetable plants, especially potato plants. They help to ward off pests as they rot down. It has a similar effect to rhubarb pest spray, but is quicker to do. It appears to be especially good against soil-borne pests, such as carrot fly and potato grub.

Early potatoes, such as Jersey Bennes, can be harvested once they begin to flower. Get your first meal by feeling around under the soil for good-sized tubers. Smaller tubers can be left to continue growing. Potatoes grown to store shouldn't be harvested until all the green leafy growth has died down. This makes the skin of the potato firm, which allows them to be stored. I always get the kids to harvest the potatoes – the digging turns it from harvesting into a treasure hunt.

Small-space growing

Grow potatoes in stacked tyres or large pots. Place 20 cm of compost in the bottom of a recycled car tyre (you can normally get these free from any tyre service) or large pot. Place three sprouted seed potatoes onto the compost and cover with another 20 cm of compost. As the plants grow, add more compost to almost cover the leaves. Add another tyre when it is needed – eventually you should have at least three tyres stacked on one another. When they are ready to harvest, just turn over the pot or dismantle the tyre stack. You will find your booty of potatoes and have compost to put on the garden.

This method of growing does require daily watering, so look at installing an irrigation system to make life easy. A soaker hose coiled up inside the tyres works well.

Growing potatoes in containers prevents rogue potato plants from popping up in your garden for years to come!

To increase your yield from a small garden space, interplant potatoes with shallow-rooted plants such as lettuce, herbs and edible flowers. These can be harvested before the potatoes have matured.

Companion plants

Grow with peas, beans, cabbage, sweet corn, eggplants, nasturtium and marigolds. Avoid growing near cucumbers, sunflowers, tomatoes and rosemary.

Peas and potatoes make good vegetable bed mates. Perhaps this is why they taste so good together.

GARLIC

Garlic is the base to so many meals that it makes sense to grow it organically. Supermarket garlic is normally Chinese grown, and has been fumigated and dipped in who knows what prior to getting to the shop. Homegrown garlic is sticky, sweet and pungent, and once you have cooked with it you will never want to go back to the inferior product. There's no excuse – it's really easy to grow.

TOP TIP

Rub freshly cut garlic on abrasions, pimples and skin infections as an antiseptic.

Buy garlic to grow from garden centres. Or save money by buying organic New Zealand-grown garlic from your local farmers' market – this locally grown garlic will still have the roots attached to the bulb. (Chinese garlic will not grow, as it has been rendered dead from all the fumigating.) Separate the individual cloves and grow the largest, plumpest ones. The smaller ones can be used in you next spag bol!

TOP TIP

To remove the odour of garlic, onions or fish from your hands, rub your hands with baking soda and water.

Garlic is traditionally planted on the shortest day and harvested on the longest day, but I often plant it in late autumn. Plant the individual cloves with the pointy end up, 5 cm deep and 10 cm apart. Cover the area in a thick layer of mulch, such as straw, to keep the area weed free – garlic does not like competition from weeds. That's all you need to do until it is ready to harvest, although if you want lovely extra-fat bulbs, feed the plants some liquid fertiliser every three weeks. If any plant produces a seedhead, cut this off, as you want all the plant's energy going into the formation of the bulb. Harvest in the middle of summer when at least half the leaf has turned brown. Hang the bulbs to dry, or get artistic and try plaiting plants together like the French do.

Mulch your garlic well as it does not like weeds growing around it. If any flower heads develop, cut them off. Garlic is ready to harvest when at least half of the plant has turned yellow.

The saying goes 'plant garlic on the shortest day and harvest on the longest'. After harvesting, I always let my garlic sit in the sun for a few days so the skin hardens, before taking it inside to store.

Small-space growing

Grow garlic in any pot or trough. Roof guttering from a house works really well. Keep well watered during the hot months.

Companion planting

Garlic likes growing with roses, so why not underplant your rose garden with garlic? It would be a great use of space. Garlic also likes growing near apples and peaches. Keep it well away from peas, beans, cabbages and strawberries.

ONIONS

Onions, like garlic, form the base of so many dishes that it's a good idea to grow it organically. Sow from seed or buy seedlings. Different varieties can be sown in spring or autumn. Add compost before sowing. If you sow seeds directly in early spring, thin the seedlings and use as spring onions in salads. When transplanting onions, don't plant too deeply as you want to see as much of the white of the stem above the ground as possible. Cut the tops off and water well until established.

Onions don't like competition from weeds, so mulch well. Water regularly until the bulb has reached near maximum size, then stop all watering to help dry the bulb. A scattering of wood ash will give added protection from pests.

Onions are ready to harvest once the tops fall over. Pull them up and leave on the soil surface to dry, in a position where the sun won't cook them. Pull off the stem once they are completely dry – normally about a week of sunny weather should do this. Use any damaged or thick stem onions first. Hang in a cool, dry place, such as a garage. Plait them or store in suspended pantyhose.

Onions drying in the sun.

TOP TIP

To prevent crying when slicing onions, place the onion in the freezer for 30 minutes before slicing.

Small-space growing

Grow onions in any pot.

Companion planting

Grow with carrots, as the smell of onion keeps carrot fly away. Onions also grow well near beetroot, silver beet and lettuce.

SPRING ONIONS

Grown from seed, spring onions can be available year round in any temperate garden. They are great in salads or as a garnish. They don't tend to bolt in warm weather, and there are many varieties to try, such as red bunching, which has a bright red stem. Sow seeds into punnets, and once the seedlings are large enough to handle, transplant them into the garden with a good quantity of compost. Plant 5 cm apart. They rarely suffer from diseases or pests.

Cut the tops off spring onions and they will keep growing and produce more stems.

Red bunching spring onions look great in salads.

Small-space growing

Grow in pots, or underplant around a larger established pot plant. Sow in a hanging basket with trailing plants such as cherry tomatoes or peas.

Companion planting

Grow with carrots, beetroot, silver beet and lettuce.

SWEET CORN

Homegrown sweet corn picked fresh and put straight into boiling water is hard to beat for taste and sweetness. These days, commercial corn is mostly genetically modified. Large conglomerates own all hybrid seeds and have developed terminator genes to make a crop 'commit suicide' after one generation. In this way these companies maintain all rights to the purchase of seeds.

So it makes sense for the home grower to grow heirloom varieties of sweet corn.

Plant seeds directly into the soil in spring, when all risk of frost is over (or you can plant in a cloche (a small tunnel house made of clear plastic) to get a head start). Plant in blocks, at around 10 cm apart, as corn is wind pollinated and plants need to be close to the next plant to produce well. Protect the developing seeds from birds by covering the area with netting. Water well as the tassels at the top of the plant form. The male flower is produced first, at the top of the plant. Shake the corn stem whenever you're passing to encourage pollen to float down onto the female part, which becomes the corncob. The corn is ready to be harvested once the tassel turns dark brown.

When corn has produced a top flower, give each plant a good shake whenever you're passing. This helps to pollinate the developing corncobs.

Once all corn has been harvested, dig the plant into the garden. This returns important carbon into the soil. Sweet corn takes a lot of nitrogen from the soil, so plant peas or beans as a following crop to replace it.

Small-space gardening

Sweet corn can be planted into a deep trough on a patio or apartment balcony to form an edible, living screen for privacy. The wind you get on a high apartment balcony will help with pollination, but you may find you need to support plants with stakes, or mound up the root area for extra support. Grow climbing beans, baby cucumbers or nasturtiums around base of plants – they will use the corn stalks as supports to grow on.

Companion planting

Plant near broad beans, potatoes, melons and cucumber. Sweet corn will lure away tomato plant pests if planted nearby.

BROAD BEANS

Broad beans have been given a bad rap by our grandmothers, who served up old, grey, bitter, wrinkly things that had been boiled for far too long. Broad beans, if picked young, are like giant, sweet, fat peas. I lightly steam the podded beans, allow them to cool, and then nick the outer skin with a knife and squeeze out the green bean. It's time consuming, but well worth the effort for your taste buds. Give them a second chance – they are well worth it.

Sow seeds in autumn, winter and early spring. Soak the seeds in water overnight then sow directly into the soil, 15 cm apart, 5 cm deep, with the seed scar downwards. Nip the tops out (nice in a stir-fry or salad) to encourage the plant to bush, creating a shorter, bushier plant. The plants will need staking – use tall canes at either end of the rows, and sturdy twine. Alternatively, when planting, push in cut branches on an angle to provide support as the plants grow. Don't

water the plants unless the weather is very dry, to avoid excessive foliage at the expense of flowers. When they are flowering, water lightly around the roots. Water at this time encourages a good number of pods to develop, at a good size. Pick the pods regularly to encourage a heavy crop.

Bees, especially bumblebees, provide the pollination, so plant nectar flowers such as lavender and echinacea nearby to encourage them.

After shelling, throw the pods back onto the garden as organic mulch.

Bees will help to pollinate your broad beans. The flowers can be picked for salads.

Broad beans come in their very own cleverly designed packaging.

Broad beans are nitrogen fixing. This means that they collect nitrogen from the air and store it in the nodules of their roots. If you look closely at the roots you can see white bumps. These are the nitrogen-filled nodules, and they are released back into the soil when the plant rots down, replacing precious nitrogen. Even if you decide you still hate eating broad beans, they can be dug into the soil as an important nitrogen-releasing green crop.

These little white bumps are full of important nitrogen. All plants need nitrogen for growth. Let these roots rot in your garden, releasing the nitrogen for other plants to use.

Small-space gardening

Dwarf broad beans can be grown in pots in any sunny position on a balcony or terrace. Tall cultivars could be used as a living screen when grown in a row of deep pots. There are several dwarf varieties that don't require strong staking, such as Coles Dwarf – this variety only grows to around one metre.

Companion planting

Broad beans and potatoes planted next to each other will inhibit pests. They also enjoy the company of carrots, cabbage, lettuce, peas, parsley and cauliflower. Broad beans enjoy growing with silver beet as this plant shades the soil. Avoid growing next to onions, garlic and fennel.

TOMATOES

Shop-bought tomatoes have been bred to be uniform in colour and form, and to have a hard skin that allows them to be shipped many miles to the consumer. Less thought has been given to their actual taste – needless to say they have little! Homegrown tomatoes are vine ripened in the summer sun, and when you bite into one you can literally taste this.

Growing tomatoes is dependent on the incidence of frosts in your region. Plant out seedlings once all chance of frost has passed, or use a cloche made from plastic drink bottles. These are easily removed as the plant grows.

TOP TIP

Save your empty but unrinsed milk bottles. Fill with water and pour over tomato plants. The residual milk helps to combat fungal disease, and the calcium in the milk feeds the plants.

There are countless varieties of tomato plants and tomatoes: dwarf or tall, small or large, oval or round; red, yellow or even purple. Some varieties are good for salads, and others are best for bottling and making into pasta sauce.

Half the fun of growing your own is trying the different heirloom and modern varieties. My suggestion is to grow a combination of both – you can then be assured of a good bounty of tomatoes that are best suited to your region. Modern varieties can be bought at any garden centre as seedlings; heirlooms are becoming easier to find through your garden centre, farmers' market, seedling grower or mail-order seed catalogues. If you are totally new to growing tomatoes, start with dwarf (cherry) tomatoes, as they are extremely easy, require no pruning or staking and are heavy fruiters. They look great through a salad or pasta dish or added as a pizza topping.

Plant tomatoes with a generous side helping of compost. One gardener I know swears by putting a tablespoon of milk powder around the roots at the time of planting. Another great trick, shared with me by a Taranaki grower, is to tie a length of copper wire loosely round the stem when the plant is around 40 cm tall. The copper will protect the plant from disease and encourage healthy growth.

A length of copper wire threaded through the tomato stem provides natural protection against pests and diseases. They can be reused every year.

Cherry tomatoes are perhaps the easiest to grow. Plant them in a pot, or let them trail over a garden wall or the edge of your raised bed.

Tall varieties need about 50 cm between each plant. Water until the small plants are well established, and then regularly when fruit is forming. When flowers are forming, feed with a liquid tea or worm wees (see page 123). The time from planting to harvest is generally three months. Tall varieties will need staking.

A recent study has shown that using red plastic mulch can boost yields. This may be worth trying. If you have any red plastic bags, lay them as a mat around each plant.

You can pinch out the lateral shoots to encourage a tall strong plant; alternatively, the permaculture way is to stake the plant and leave it alone. With this method the fruit forms in the middle of the plant, and the leafy growth protects it from birds and the weather. The individual tomatoes may not be as big but the crop is large. From three plants I regularly get a bucket of fruit every week throughout the season.

TOP TIP

Tomatoes and potatoes are from the same family and carry the same diseases. Don't plant potatoes where tomatoes have recently grown, and vice versa.

At the end of the growing season, if you still have unripe tomatoes on your plant, hang the entire plant upside down in a garage or shed and the tomatoes will ripen.

Small-space growing

Grow dwarf (cherry) tomatoes in hanging baskets. Or make your own hanging planter from a 20-litre paint bucket or similar: cut a hole in the base and plant a tomato plant into this hole so that it is hanging upside down out of the bucket. Fill the bucket with good-quality potting mix with added water-holding crystals. You could plant basil in the top of the bucket. Hang it by the handle in a sunny spot. You will need to water the container regularly, as the plants grow and use up all the available growing space. The tomatoes will trail down, making them easy to pick. It also prevents them rotting, as happens when they are grown on the ground. Cherry tomatoes can also be grown on a windowsill with a small bamboo stake to keep them upright.

Grow all varieties of tomatoes in a grow bag or a potting mix bag. These are basically 40-litre plastic bags full of potting mix .You can even buy specialised potting mix bags that are formulated for growing tomatoes, with the correct ratio of nutrients. The idea is to cut several evenly spaced holes (about two for tall varieties or four for dwarf types), large enough to plant seedlings into. The tomatoes can grow in this bag and the potting mix

can afterwards be reused for pots or put into the garden. Place the tomatoes in their grow bags in a sunny spot against a wall and keep watered. On a warm and sunny apartment balcony, you may find your tomato-growing season will be extended because of the warmth that radiates off the hard surfaces, and because there is no risk of frosts.

Make use of a balcony railing by trailing tomatoes along this structure instead of staking with canes. Tie the tomato vines with soft twine or old pantyhose cut into strips.

Tomatoes grown high up on an apartment balcony or in a busy city may need help with pollination, as bees and other insects may be absent. Use a soft artist's brush to gently brush mature flowers. This spreads pollen and develops fruit.

Grafted tomatoes (super toms) are vigorous, heavy-cropping types and are a good choice if you only have room for one or two plants.

Companion planting

Basil is the obvious companion for tomatoes, but also plant near asparagus, celery, carrots, sweet corn and garlic. Avoid rosemary, potatoes, fennel and dill.

DWARF AND RUNNER BEANS

Bean seeds can be planted directly into the soil from spring through to late summer, once the soil temperature is around 15°C. They like a warm, moist soil, but aren't fussy about nutrient levels as they are nitrogen fixers. Runner beans can be planted in the same position each year – they will grow like a perennial and come up each year in late spring. Refresh the soil with compost and plant

Dwarf bean flowers and developing beans.

Scarlet runner beans produce vibrant red flowers over summer. Bees love them. They are a vigorous climber so require a strong support structure. They put on a spectacular show, so why not grow them in your flower garden?

5 cm deep and 10 cm apart. Runner beans will need support as they can grow up to three metres in height. Use a bamboo tepee or climbing frame.

The most common cause of failure is too much moisture during germination, as this can rot the seed. Don't water until you can see shoots above the ground, then start watering regularly around the root zone to encourage heavy cropping. Pick regularly to encourage a bountiful but tender-tasting crop. Sow seed every month to ensure a continual supply over summer.

Beans don't like wind, so mound soil around the stem if you experience high winds.

Once the harvest has ended, dig the plants into the soil to return the nitrogen. Bean seeds can easily be collected for next year: let a few of the largest beans dry on the plant until they are brown and completely dry. Then shell the beans and place them in a dry, dark container or paper bag, and label. Re-sow next year for a totally self-sufficient crop.

TOP TIP

Peel vegetables on a sheet of newspaper. When finished, roll it all up together and throw it in the compost.

Small-space growing

Plant dwarf beans in a window box or pot. Dwarf beans can also be planted under larger plants in pots. Climbing beans could be grown in a pot next to a trellis or railing. If you are growing corn at the same time, plant runner beans at the base – they will scramble up the corn.

Companion plants

Dwarf beans, beetroot and potatoes planted in alternative rows will help keep each other happy. Zinnias, garlic, chives and sunflowers are also good neighbours.

TOP TIP

Store vegetables in paper bags in the fridge – they will last longer and stay fresh.

Picking a few of the young tender leaves for salads will not compromise your beetroot crop.

BEETROOT

Originally a seaside plant, beetroot enjoys salty, sandy conditions, but luckily it is easy to grow in most other situations. Beetroot is frost hardy, but sow seeds in spring through to autumn. Three to four seeds are encased within a corky, knobbly capsule. Soak the seeds overnight.

Each plant needs about 8 cm of space to develop. Beetroot likes a sunny position and rich soil, but not fresh manure. Though it is a tough plant it appreciates water during dry periods. Keep the area well weeded. As the plant is growing you can carefully pick several of the developing leaves to use in salads.

The beetroot forms at the soil's surface, so it is easy to see when it is big enough to harvest. If you keep chickens or rabbits, feed them the leaves – they love them.

Small-space growing

Plant seeds directly into pots or window boxes. Plant between established flowering plants, as the leaves are very attractive in their own right.

Companion plants

Beetroot grows well near onions, silver beet, cabbage and dwarf beans.

It pays not to 'over-love' your beets. Treat them mean and they will reward you with jumbo beetroot for your burgers!

MESCLUN MIX

This seed mixture contains lettuce, rocket, endive, mustard, chicory and beets, to name a few. Why pay money for fancy shop-bought mesclun mixes when you can grow the same product at home organically? This seed mixture can be grown from spring through to autumn. Prepare the soil by lightly digging and firming – press the soil with the palm of your hand so that it is level. Sprinkle the seed mix, press into the soil and water with a sprinkler. In summer the seed will germinate within 10 days. Keep well watered and protect from slugs and snails. Harvest by cutting with scissors whenever you need fresh salad. The leaves will regrow several times. Regular harvesting will prevent the crop bolting and going to seed, as it can do during the hot summers.

Small-space gardening

Because mesclun is shallow rooted, you can grow it in recycled guttering. You could even suspend this outside a sunny window as a mini window box. Any flat pot that has a large surface area would work well. Better still, have two containers so that one is germinating while you are harvesting the other. This way you can have fresh salad greens throughout the growing season.

Use mesclun regularly by cutting leaves with scissors. In hot summers, grow it under taller crops so it has shade. This will prevent it bolting to seed in the heat.

Companion plants

Grow near beetroot, cabbages, radishes and marigolds.

LEEKS

Leeks are really useful to have in the garden. When young they can be used like spring onions, and they will happily sit in the garden throughout winter. Sow seeds in seed trays in spring through to autumn, and, when they are big enough to handle, plant out in soil that is free draining and has compost or wood ash added. Prior to planting the seedlings, cut the tops back to around 5 cm and trim the roots to the same length. Plant deeply in the soil so that the tops are still showing. This encourages long white stems. Leeks benefit from a monthly liquid feed.

When they are fully grown and you want the garden space for another crop, you can pull the leek plants out and heel them in somewhere else – dig a trench, place the leeks into it and lightly backfill the soil. The leeks will happily sit there until needed in the kitchen.

Leeks are a versatile plant to have in your garden. Use in place of onions in any dish.

Small-space gardening

Plant in any deep pot, or dot plants around any established patio garden – their upright habit makes a statement with established plants.

Companion planting

Leeks like carrots, peas and calendula.

SPINACH AND SILVER BEET

Both of these plants are easy to grow as long as the weather is not too hot. Both like rich soil and constant moisture. Sow seeds directly into the planting position in late summer, about 2 cm deep and 5 cm apart. As they grow, thin the plants to around 15 cm apart. Harvest outer leaves as needed. Chickens consider these plants as caviar and will devour them within seconds. They will thank you with dark orange yolks.

You could try growing these plants in summer if you have a shady area, or perhaps around the back of a trellis used for another crop. Another way to provide shade is to plant on the south side of tall plants such as sweet corn.

Rainbow silver beet will grow for several months. Harvest the outer leaves as needed. The stem colours make this an attractive plant to grow in an ornamental garden.

Small-space gardening

You could grow spinach as a border for other crops. Rainbow silver beet, with its many-coloured stems, looks very ornamental growing in a pot or along a path.

Companion planting

Onions and beetroot are their favourite companions.

CARROTS

Carrots can be tricky to grow, but the taste of a fresh carrot pulled straight from the garden is hard to beat. Carrots don't transplant well, so you must sow directly into the soil. For the best germination results use fresh seed. The tiny seeds are best mixed with some sand or used coffee grounds, which stop you from sowing them too thickly. Sow onto well-worked soil, but not onto thick mulch. Pat down but do not cover with soil. It is important to keep the area constantly moist until the carrots germinate. This can be as long as three weeks. Try covering the area with a damp hessian sack between watering to keep moist. Carrots are a cool season crop – when grown in hot weather they are bitter and woody. Don't plant when the season is changing from cool to warm, as this will cause the plant to bolt to seed. Plant when the days are becoming cooler and shorter. I prefer to grow baby carrots as they only take a few months. If you want long carrots, avoid planting in soil with rocks or large stones, as obstacles like this produce crooked and forked carrots.

Kids love harvesting carrots.

Small-space gardening

Plant in pots or troughs mixed with radish seed. Carrots are slow to germinate, but the radish will pop up within a couple of days, marking the area and breaking the surface for the delicate carrot seedlings. When the radishes are ready to harvest, the carrots will still be very small. This way you will get two crops from the one space. Plant baby carrots in containers and re-sow every two weeks. This way you will have several crops coming along at different times in the same container.

Companion planting

Carrots grow well with peas, radishes, lettuce, chives, onions and leeks. Try a mixed planting of leeks and carrot seeds. The carrots will be ready to harvest before the leeks, which will act as protection against the carrot fly.

TOP TIP

Female cabbage white butterflies are very territorial. To deter them, place half eggshells (shell up) on small sticks amongst your brassica to mimic white butterflies. Another idea is to cut out shapes of butterflies from ice-cream lids and stick on your brassica plants.

BROCCOLI

Broccoli likes rich soil and benefits from mulch and a seaweed brew, or compost containing seaweed. Broccoli plants do best when the season is not too hot, as hot weather often makes the plant bolt to seed. Plant out seedlings about 30 cm apart. To protect these succulent seedlings from snails and slugs, put a tin can (or takeaway coffee cup) with the bottom cut out over the plant. Carefully push the can over the plant and into the soil. This prevents these pests chomping at the stems. Remove as the plant grows. When you cut the central head off the plant, do so at an angle so that the stem sheds water, preventing rotting. Smaller side shoots will grow, and these can be harvested.

Small-space gardening

Broccoli will grow in any medium-sized pot. Use a good-quality potting mix mixed with compost, and keep well watered in the sun. These plants are greedy feeders and need lots of compost or liquid fertiliser.

Companion planting

Broccoli belongs to the cabbage family, so it has the same property of stunting the growth of strawberries if planted next to them.

TOP TIP

Lay large rhubarb leaves over the top of cabbages and cauliflowers to protect from insect attacks. The scent of the rhubarb helps to disguise and deter.

PUMPKIN, CUCUMBERS, COURGETTES, SCALLOPINI AND SQUASH (CUCURBITS)

I have included these plants together as they are all very easy to grow and enjoy similar growing conditions. The first touch of frost will kill these plants, but nothing else will. Plant in early summer. If you have a compost bin or worm farm you may find pumpkin seedlings sprouting in these – use them for your crop. These plants will quickly overrun your garden so don't turn your back on them, ever! Plant in deeply worked soil after adding lots of compost. They need plenty of water (preferably in the morning, to prevent fungal diseases). Provide good drainage and thick mulch, as they have surface roots. If you have clay soil, mix in lots of sand to increase the water-draining properties. Bees will pollinate these plants, but if you don't have any bees, hand-pollinate the flowers by transferring pollen with a small paintbrush. Encourage bees to visit by planting lavender, borage or basil that has gone to flower nearby.

If you wish to store pumpkins or squash over winter, wait for the outer shell to harden and then cut off the vine leaving about 5 cm of stem. Store in a cool dry place.

Small-space gardening

These plants are large sprawling creatures by nature, so in a small space the only option is probably to go up. Plant a seedling next to a strong trellis and train the plant upwards. As the plant grows, tie the stems onto the trellis using strong ties. The forming fruit needs to be supported or it will break from the plant. Use net bags such as those that onions come in. Place the growing fruit in the bag and tie the bag to the trellis. Another idea (which would become a talking point) is to use an old bra. Tie the bra straps onto the trellis and support the pumpkin or squash in the cups!

Alternatively, plant in a large wooden barrel and let the plants spill over and across the ground as they grow.

As these plants are all shallow rooting, don't try to grow anything else around the stem.

Companion planting

Cucumbers are very friendly plants. They get on with potatoes, celery, lettuce, beans and cabbages. They especially like sunflowers and sweet corn, as these plants provide some welcome shade in summer.

Pumpkins and squash also enjoy the company of sweet corn, but they do not grow well near potatoes.

Freshly picked scallopini and yellow courgettes.
I sell the scallopini to the kids as 'mini flying saucers'.
They bite into them at dinnertime, looking for aliens.

CHAPTER FOUR

GROWING FRUIT

MANY PEOPLE THINK IT'S IMPOSSIBLE TO HAVE AN ORCHARD IN THE CITY, BUT THERE ARE MANY CLEVER WAYS OF CRAMMING FRUIT-BEARING PLANTS INTO A SMALL SPACE. THE SECRET IS TO CHOOSE DWARF FRUIT TREES. DEPENDING ON THE VARIETY AND SPECIES, THESE ONLY GROW TO ABOUT TWO METRES TALL. NOT ONLY DO THEY SAVE SPACE, BUT THEY ALSO COST LESS TO SPRAY, WATER AND FERTILISE.

The maypole apple tree grows to around two metres tall. If you want a formal garden, consider planting these trees in straight rows. Not only will you have that calm, formal space, but also spring blossom, autumn colour and some fruit to consume.

CREATING A MINI URBAN ORCHARD

A good example is the maypole apple tree, which grows like a telegraph pole, taking up little lateral space. The fruit develop off the main trunk. These shapely trees look wonderful incorporated into a formal courtyard design.

Another good use of space is to grow espalier fruit trees (these are trained so their branches grow horizontally along wire) on a boundary fence or building wall. Espaliered trees take up little room and fruit heavily because of their regular pruning. You can also grow climbing fruit plants over trellis, fences, constructed arbours and pergolas.

Plant hazelnut, mandarin or feijoa trees as hedges, and plant macadamia, quince or plum trees as ornamental trees to provide shade and structure.

Next time you're planning on planting a hedge, consider an edible variety. A feijoa hedge is fast growing, evergreen, and can be clipped. The fruit can be eaten fresh or frozen. I make feijoa crumble, feijoa ice cream, and, when the glut is really on, feijoa wine! If you plant several different varieties they will cross-pollinate, and you are guaranteed a bumper crop each year.

Quince trees are a good choice for a small garden as they only grow to around three metres tall. The fruit, which is rarely found for sale in shops, can be used to make jelly, pies and preserves, or can be cooked with meat.

A dwarf peach tree only grows to around one metre high. It has a very formal appearance so looks great in a large pot or formal garden. As with all stone fruit you need to follow a spray programme to keep the tree healthy. Expect to harvest from half to one bucket of normal-sized fruit each year.

It is very important to choose fruit trees that are suited to your climate (see table, page 73). For example, if your winters are warm, don't try to grow apricots as they require a cold winter to develop fruit.

Buy multi-grafted trees – these have several varieties on one plant. This means they can pollinate each other, and you can enjoy both early and late-season fruit from the same tree.

Grow named varieties of fruit, rather than attempting to grow your own trees from pips. Pip-grown seedlings can be unreliable and may never successfully bear fruit. Choose organic old-fashioned varieties, as they generally grow better in the home garden and don't require such a rigorous spray programme as some of the commercial varieties.

Keep the plant labels on your trees so you can remember what they are.

FRUIT VARIETIES: WINTER TEMPERATURE TOLERANCE

Mild winters: semi-tropical climate, warm and humid, frosts are rare Northland, Auckland, Waikato; other coastal areas	Moderately cold winters: frosts during winter, hot dry summers Bay of Plenty, Hawke's Bay, New Plymouth, Wellington, Nelson	Very cold winters: regular frost, snow that sometimes settles for a short time, cool in spring and autumn, warm summers Rest of the South Island
Coffee	Cherries: Compact Stella, Dawson	Peaches
Tamarillos	Olives	Nectarines
Almonds: Garden Prince	Figs	Apples
Passion fruit	Almonds	Pears
Bananas	Cocktail kiwifruit	Quince
Feijoas	Avocados: Hass are the most frost tolerant	Plums: European
Figs	Limes – only in warm, frost-free spots	Strawberries
Olives	New Zealand grapefruit and Wheeny grapefruit	Gooseberries
Kiwifruit	Meyer lemons	Loganberries
Mountain pawpaws	Olives	Boysenberries
Avocados	Peaches	Blueberries
Plums: only Japanese plums (*Prunus salicina*) and low-chill varieties like Satsuma, Burbank, Doris	Nectarines	Apricots
Mandarins	Apples	Raspberries
Limes: Tahitian and Mexican	Apricots: Sundrop	Currants
Grapefruit	Pears	Grapes
Lemons	Quinces	Mulberries
Peaches	Plums	Walnuts
Nectarines: Fantasia	Strawberries	Hazelnuts
Apples	Gooseberries	
Pears	Loganberries	
Quinces	Boysenberries	
Strawberries	Raspberries	
Blueberries	Blueberries	
Walnuts	Currants	
Grapes	Hazelnuts	
Mulberries	Pecans	
Macadamia	Grapes	
Pepinos	Mulberries	
	Walnuts	

TOP TIP

Place unripe stone fruit in paper bags with other ripe fruit. They will quickly ripen.

To save money, purchase bare-rooted fruit trees in winter. They are cost effective because you don't pay for the transportation and handling of heavy pots. Bare-rooted trees are only available in winter when the plant is dormant. Sometimes you need to pre-order them from nurseries in summer and autumn.

Picking apples after school.

TOP TIP

Shared by Fulford, Green Community Forum

To treat scratches on wooden furniture, cut a fresh walnut in half and gently rub the scratched surface in a circular motion. The walnut oils will make the scratch disappear.

When purchasing your trees, check whether they are self-fertile or require another variety to pollinate the flowers. If you are planting for pollination, position the pollinator no more than 30 m away so the bees don't have too far to travel. Look over the fence and around your neighbourhood – your neighbour may have a pollinator in their garden.

Encourage bees to visit by planting bee-attracting flowers; you could even set up a hive within the orchard space.

If you have room to grow several types of fruit tree, group similar varieties together. For example, plant all pip fruit trees together and all stone fruit trees together, and a citrus grove in another area. This allows you to manage your similar trees together whether spraying, pruning or fertilising.

TOP TIP

Never dig under fruit trees.
They have fine surface feeder roots.

CHOOSING AND PLANTING TREES

I recommend buying two-year-old trees rather than older and larger four- or five-year-old trees. I have found that these older trees never do very well once planted in the garden. The shock of transplanting can often make them sit and sulk. Younger trees quickly settle in and will outgrow an older tree, which means they will start producing sooner.

Look for a plant that has clean, green, healthy-looking leaf growth. Avoid buying anything with blotchy, spotty or wrinkled leaves. Check the trunk where the graft is. This normally looks like a raised collar of bark around the trunk, just above the soil. Make sure there is no growth below this graft site. Also check the soil in the pot – make sure there are no weeds, especially oxalis, and that the soil is damp. This is a good indication that the plant has been well cared for during its time at the nursery.

Turn the pot on its side and see if there are any roots growing out of the drainage holes. This can mean the plant is root bound and should have been repotted into a larger pot. Root-bound trees have roots that have been forced to grow in a cramped pot and often spiral around on themselves. A root-bound tree can take longer to establish important feeder roots and the larger roots that secure the plant in the soil.

For citrus trees, choose a tree with healthy, rounded, vigorously growing foliage. Choose pip and stone fruit trees that have a strong straight central trunk. Always make sure the tree has an attached label so you are sure of the variety. Although it is tempting to buy trees that already have fruit on, this fruit needs to be removed at time of planting or it will weaken the tree: all a new tree's energy needs to go towards developing a strong root structure.

The best time to plant trees is in autumn or early winter. This gives the roots plenty of time to re-establish before the hot, dry conditions of summer. Soil temperatures are generally warmer during autumn than in spring, and soil moisture levels are often more suitable for planting. There are usually fewer drying winds at this time of year.

PLANTING A TREE: A STEP-BY-STEP GUIDE

Step 1: Dig the hole

Dig the hole at least twice the width and depth of the tree's container. Make the hole square rather than round – this prevents the roots from following the internal shape of the hole and spiralling around.

Dig a square-sided hole to plant your tree or shrub.

Step 2: Take the tree out of its container

Water the tree and hole deeply, then lay the tree on its side and pull it out of the container. Don't use the trunk to pull out the tree as this can harm the roots. If the roots are pot bound, tease them out by hand or make two or three vertical cuts about two centimetres deep from the top of the root ball to the bottom with a sharp knife.

Step 3: Insert a stake (or two)

Place a stake (two is better) in the planting hole. Put stakes outside the root ball area of the tree to prevent root damage. If you're using just one stake, place this on the side of the prevailing wind. Hammer in until very firm. Tree ties can be bought from nurseries, or make your own from pantyhose or webbing.

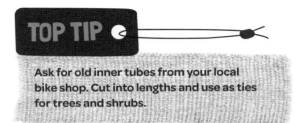

Ask for old inner tubes from your local bike shop. Cut into lengths and use as ties for trees and shrubs.

Step 4: Plant your tree

Place the tree in the prepared hole, making sure the top of the soil in the container is at the same level as the ground. If you are using the milk bottle watering system (see page 77), place the bottle in the hole now. Backfill the topsoil, firming it around the tree ball with the heel of your boot. If you're using a slow-release fertiliser, or compost, apply it now around the top of the root ball. Apply a thick layer of mulch around the base of the tree, being careful not to let it touch the trunk as this can cause rotting or fungal diseases.

Step 5: Aftercare

Keep your tree well irrigated for the first year, and regularly check stakes to ensure they are supporting the tree. Stakes only need to remain on the tree for two years, but need to be checked to ensure that they are still providing support, and that the ties haven't become too tight.

Shared by Kayo, Green Community Forum

A recent overseas study has shown that giving newly planted trees some sugar helps develop a strong root system and ward off pests and diseases. The recommended ratio is three tablespoons of sugar to one litre of water.

CARING FOR YOUR FRUIT TREE

Mulch the root area with compost to keep grass and weeds from growing, and keep the tree well watered during dry periods. Remove any fruit that forms in the first year.

For smaller and minor pruning work, it is essential to use clean and sharp pruning tools. Remove any dead or diseased branches as soon as you notice them. When you're cutting, do not leave any snags, and make sure the cut is as close to the main branch or trunk as possible. If the branch to be removed is larger than three centimetres in diameter, always make an undercut with your pruning saw. This avoids tearing the bark after cutting.

It is important, especially in younger trees, to maintain a leader. This is the upright, vertical growing tip. If the leader becomes damaged, you need to prune back to the next outside bud to encourage new growth. In time this growth should establish as the new leader.

It's a good idea to cover the pruning cut with a pruning paint. (You can buy special pruning paint, but I use any water-based paint I have in the garage.) This protects the tree from disease. Check this area of the tree from time to time to ensure it is callusing over and free from decay.

An idea to steal: The milk bottle watering system

Newly transplanted trees need 15 litres of water a week to establish a good root system. Traditional watering methods often produce run-off or take time as we stand with hose in hand. Here's an idea for an inexpensive homemade system that uses recycled materials to create a watering device.

- You need a plastic two- or three-litre milk container, a rubber band and an empty onion bag.

- Poke two to three fine holes in the bottom of the milk bottle.

- Cut a circle of onion-bag netting and fasten it over the opening of the container with the rubber band. This will keep out leaves, insects and soil.

- Dig a hole next to the tree, making sure not to damage its roots, and place the container inside the hole. The neck of the milk bottle should be a fraction higher than the ground. Firm the soil around the milk bottle.

- Fill the container with water. Refill the bottle as necessary: small trees need 15 litres a week; larger ones need 30 litres a week. Space the watering over the week so that the plant receives moisture as evenly and steadily as possible.

- You can liquid feed the tree with compost tea or worm wees (see page 123).

- After a few years, remove the milk bottle and fill in the hole with compost.

A milk bottle waterer makes it easy to irrigate trees over a hot summer, delivering water straight to the tree's roots. Place one in the planting hole when you're planting your tree.

TOP FRUIT TO GROW IN AN URBAN GARDEN

APPLES

Everyone loves apples, especially me. I have about ten different varieties growing in our garden.

Varieties fruit at different times – some in January, and some as late as May. So if you're clever you can plant several different types and enjoy fresh apples for nearly six months of the year.

Grow apples in moist fertile soil to get them established quickly. Stake them well at planting time. Once mature they are as tough as old boots and will tolerate neglect. Apple trees – any fruit trees for that matter – don't like grass growing around their trunk, so weed or apply a mulch layer around the drip zone. Try wool dags or bark mulch. Alternatively, plant beneficial herbs around the tree. These can include comfrey, borage, spring bulbs and alyssum. These plants keep the grass down, attract bees for pollination and mine minerals from the soil for the tree to use.

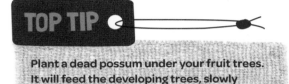

TOP TIP

Plant a dead possum under your fruit trees. It will feed the developing trees, slowly providing a great fertiliser.

I don't bother pruning my apple trees (apart from the espaliered ones). With an unpruned apple tree, the fruit is protected from birds and ripens in stages – perfect for home gardeners that don't want a glut in one day. If your tree becomes too messy, prune any thin straggly growth every few years.

New apples developing on a tree. An apple is ready to be eaten when it comes off in your hand with a gentle pull.

Best varieties to grow

I grow heritage types of apples – I find that they don't need as much spraying and their taste is wonderful. The new Rezista varieties are also a good choice, as they have been bred to be resistant to black spot and other fungal problems.

Here is a list of apple varieties I have had success growing in my garden organically.

- **Initial:** early season apple that is sweet, red and crunchy. It has a naturally high resistance to disease.

- **Hetlina:** this apple has high levels of antioxidants. It is an early season apple that is red and crunchy on a hig-health tree.

Four-year-old espaliered Initial apples ripening in the sun.

- **Baujade:** this is a French variety that ripens late. The apple looks and tastes like a Granny Smith. The tree grows vigorously and has lovely pink blossoms.

- **Monty's Surprise:** this is a New Zealand variety that came out tops in recent research into the cancer-fighting properties of apples. It is a huge apple, green in colour with flecks of red. It is wonderfully crisp and juicy for eating.

- **Winter Banana:** This is a late-season heritage variety. It is pale yellow with a faint blush of pink. Its taste is a combination of sweet with tart. It has a definite aroma of banana, hence the name. It makes a good cooking and dessert apple.

Where to plant apples

Try growing a hedge of dwarf apple trees along a boundary line. Or plant dwarf types in large half wine barrels. Grow one as a specimen tree on the lawn, or plant on the council verge so children can enjoy a snack when walking home from school. Espalier dwarfing types run along wire to form a living fence or to disguise an ugly wall. Plant maypole-type crab apples in a formal garden.

Rootstock and grafting explained

Most fruit trees are propagated by grafting, as they do not grow true to form from pips and stones. A cutting from the tree to be propagated is grafted onto rootstock (a similar species or variety of plant that has been chosen for disease resistance or root vigour).

This thickened band is the graft site where a dwarf pear tree has been joined to a different type of root (a quince). If you look closely, you can see that the two types of bark are different colours and textures. If any growth appears below the graft site, as it has on this pear tree, remove it. (The quince leaves growing below the rootstock look quite different to the pear leaves.)

Apple rootstock includes:

- M25: vigorous apple stock, used for traditional standard trees in orchards.
- Northern Spy: an old-fashioned rootstock well suited to clay soils. The tree grows to three metres.
- MM106: Semi-dwarf apple stock, used for a standard-sized tree.
- M9: Dwarf apple tree stock, used for dwarfs, cordons and espalier.
- M26: Semi-dwarf apple tree stock used for bushes, hedges and multiple cordons.
- M27: Very dwarf apple stock, used for container trees and stepover espalier designs.

PLUMS

A sun-warmed spray-free plum, fresh off a tree, is hard to beat. Plum trees are quite location specific, so I recommend you buy from a local nursery where they can advise which will do best in your climate. When you buy your tree, ask if it is self-fertile or needs a pollinator. If it's the latter, it will perform well if it has another variety of plum nearby to cross-pollinate. Alternatively, buy a double-grafted variety.

I grow 'Billington', which is one of the earliest red plums to ripen in summer. The fruit are dark red and richly flavoured, and don't lose their colour when you stew them. The tree crops heavily and is self-fertile.

For best results, lightly prune the tree when young to develop an open fan shape. The fruit is produced on mainly two-year-old wood. Each year prune any diseased wood or old tired branches from the middle of the tree. Cut the

A plum tree is a great choice for an urban backyard. It can grow successfully without judicious spraying, and is ornamental in its own right.

new season's growth in half; this encourages replacement spurs. (Spurs are the short stumpy shoots on which the fruit develops.) I feed my plum tree with lime, and ash from the fire (a type of homemade potash), each autumn.

TOP TIP

When spraying fruit trees, make sure you thoroughly spray all the bark as it can harbour disease.

Where to plant plums

A mature plum tree grows quite large, so allow room for it to develop. If space is an issue, you can espalier plum trees in a fan shape against a sunny wall.

Plums put up with most soils, but do best in rich, free-draining soil. They can be affected by late spring frosts, so choose a warm position in the garden. Plums also need a sunny position to help build up the sugars in the fruit. In the right sunny spot your plum tree will start producing its first crop in around three years.

TOP TIP

When planting new shrubs or trees, line the hole with several sheets of newspaper. Fill the hole with the plant and soil. The newspaper prevents water draining away too quickly and adds organic matter as it rots down.

COCKTAIL KIWIFRUIT

This plant is a native of China, Korea, Japan and Siberia. It has a similar growing habit to its hairy cousin, but the fruit are much nicer to eat as they are green, hairless and about the size of a large marble – perfect for popping into your mouth! You can eat the fruit like a grape and add to salads or desserts. My cocktail kiwifruit crop has failed to make it into the house yet, because the neighbourhood kids love to free range around the vine during March and April when the fruit is ripening.

There are male and female cocktail kiwifruit plants, and they need to be planted together. They are vines, so grow over a pergola, fence or similar support system. Plant in full sun, in fertile soil. Bees will pollinate the fruit – I plant lots of borage around the vine to attract them. Prune after fruiting. (My vine started to fruit after three years.)

The cocktail kiwifruit plant is free from problems, and the birds tend to leave it alone, even if the neighbourhood kids don't!

Cocktail kiwifruit ripening in the hot sun. In late summer, when they turn light brown and are soft to touch, they are ready to eat. When you cut them in half they look exactly like a normal kiwifruit. I often use them to decorate a pavlova. They look quirky: small, but perfectly formed.

FIGS

You rarely find fresh figs in supermarkets, which is a shame as they are delicious. A fig tree can be planted as a lawn specimen, and, in time, will create lovely summer shade and a great climbing tree for kids.

Fig trees are long-lived and low care. I do nothing to our established tree: no spraying, no pruning and no watering. However, young fig trees are susceptible to frosts. Try growing them in a container, or espalier along a building to protect them.

Fig trees also do well when planted in a large pot, such as a half wine barrel. This naturally dwarfs them but they will still fruit well.

Fig trees like free-draining soil and need sun to ripen the fruit. The length and heat of summer determines what sort of crop will result. The hotter

the better. It's important to wait for the fruit to ripen before picking, as once picked they will not ripen further. They are ready to be harvested when they feel soft to the touch. Pick them straight off the tree and straight into the mouth, skin and all. (Note that when the fruit is picked the tree excretes a white sap, which can be a slight irritant to your skin.)

It's always a race at our place to get the fruit before the birds do. Try netting smaller trees.

I grow Oakura. It produces large green fruit with firm red flesh. It has a lovely sweet flavour and the leaves are big, bold and dramatic. Try stuffing a piece of blue cheese inside a fresh fig, then wrap in bacon and cook on the barbecue.

NEW ZEALAND CRANBERRIES

This is a superb plant to grow, for so many reasons. Plant it next to patios or windows to enjoy its lovely scent, or plant as an edible hedge in place of the more standard hedges of pittosporum or griselinia. It can be clipped and used in formal gardens for topiary or in place of buxus hedges, and it can be grown in containers. You could also standardise them or use them for a very formal look. The fruit is packed with fibre and vitamins C and K.

New Zealand cranberry is an evergreen, with small shiny leaves. It looks very similar to buxus hedging. The small, pale pink flowers appear in spring. The following small, red, round fruit are delicious eaten straight from the bush. When my three-year-old discovered them, the plant was literally stripped bare. Luckily my four-year-old plant produces around a kilo of fruit. Plant New Zealand cranberries in any well-drained fertile soil. They can take the frosts and will also fruit in semi-shaded positions. Prune to shape after they have fruited, to stop them getting too straggly. I have never had to treat them for any pest or disease.

Fresh figs are delicious and often not available to buy. Eat them fresh off the tree like an apple; poach them, pickle them or make chutneys and jam to store over the year.

TOP TIP

Hang old compact mirrors or CDs in your fruit trees to scare away birds.

TOP TIP

To help remove pesticides from bought fruit and vegetables, combine four tablespoons of white vinegar and fill the sink with water. Soak the produce for a few minutes.

Websites to visit

www.waimeanurseries.co.nz
– find out the best varieties for your location and then order through your local garden centre.

www.plantsnz.co.nz
– provides a great summary of fruiting times for all fruit trees, plus an online shop.

www.ediblegarden.co.nz
– buy heritage and multi-grafted trees.

www.edible.co.nz
– information on many new and different edibles to grow in the home garden.

ORGANIC SPRAY PROGRAMME FOR FRUIT TREES

Time of year	Organic control	Uses
Late autumn: immediately after leaf fall	Full-strength Bordeaux mixture	Controls leaf curl
Late winter: when tree is dormant	Lime sulphur or Neem	Controls aphids, mites and scale
Early spring: when blossom buds are forming	Copper oxychloride or lime sulphur	Controls brown rot and bacteria
Late spring: when about two-thirds of petals have fallen and new sprouting leaves can be seen	Lime sulphur, Neem or pyrethrum (alternate all three)	Controls aphids, bacteria, brown rot and powdery mildew
Summer through autumn: after blossom fall to four weeks before harvest, at monthly intervals	• Pyrethrum, Neem or lime sulphur, OR copper and lime sulphur (don't mix) • Diatomaceous earth paint applied to trunks	• Controls aphids, caterpillars, brown rot, bacteria, powdery mildew, passion vine hopper, mealy bug, scale • Controls codling moth

CHAPTER FIVE

GROWING HERBS

NOTHING SPRUCES UP A SALAD OR A MEAL MORE THAN FRESHLY PICKED HERBS FROM YOUR GARDEN. HERBS ARE EASY TO GROW, AND GREAT FOR POTS AND PLANTERS CLOSE TO THE KITCHEN. THEY ARE MUCH BETTER TO USE IN COOKING THAN DRIED HERBS, WHICH OFTEN GIVE A BITTER TASTE TO DISHES. USE THEM FOR GARNISH, AND EVEN AS CAKE DECORATION.

A ladder planter enables you to stack herb plants in a small space.

TOP TIP

Dry fresh herbs by tying them in bundles and hanging them upside down in paper bags in a warm dry room or garage. When dry, remove the stalks and crush the leaves by rolling a glass jar or tin can over the bag. Label and store in an airtight container.

TOP CULINARY HERBS TO GROW

BASIL

No other smell reminds me more of summer than fresh basil. This tender annual likes full sun and frost-free climates. It grows best in rich, moist soil that is well drained.

There are many different varieties of basil to grow, with different tastes and leaf colour. I love the sweet or common basil. Sow it from seed in spring, once all threat of frost has passed. Sow it directly in the garden – there should be no problem with germination as long as the soil temperature has warmed to 20°C during the day. Cover the area with rich black compost to help heat the soil.

Pick the tips of your basil plants regularly to keep them bushy. Basil is a great companion plant to tomatoes.

Start picking the leaves once the plant is big enough. Pick them from the top of the plant to encourage leafy, compact growth. Small but regular pickings are best.

Feed your basil regularly with comfrey tea for lots of leaf growth, and pick off any developing seedheads to encourage more leaf growth. Towards the end of summer allow some plants to set seed. Honeybees love the white flower spikes and the resulting seed is easy to harvest. On a dry sunny day when the seed head is brown and dry, pick and store in a paper bag or envelope for next year. Remember to name the bag.

Uses

- Use the fresh leaves in salads, stir-fries and Mediterranean dishes. You can preserve in oil, vinegars or butter.

- Basil tea is reputed to be a remedy for travel sickness. Pour boiling water onto a sprig of freshly cut leaves.

- The smell of basil is said to repel flies and other insects, but you need a lot for it to be effective. A large pot plant of basil growing on the kitchen windowsill will help to keep those summer flies away.

Basil pesto recipe

- 2 cups freshly picked and washed basil leaves (if you don't have enough basil, mix with fresh parsley leaves)

- 3 cloves fresh garlic

- 1 cup pine nuts

- extra virgin olive oil to mix

Put the first three ingredients into a food processor and mix thoroughly. Add the olive oil. Will keep for two weeks when stored in the fridge.

CORIANDER

People seem to either love or hate coriander (or cilantro, as some people call it). It is spicy, and essential if you love Thai food. It's an easy herb to grow – as it's fast growing the seeds can be sown directly into the garden. However, it does have a propensity to bolt to seed in hot summers, so it's best grown in shade, perhaps behind taller vegetables or on the shady side of the house in a pot. Sow the seeds in autumn, and to ensure a long cropping season sow a few seeds every few weeks. They are quick to germinate, and you can be harvesting the young fresh leaves within five weeks. Coriander will grow in any garden soil, but avoid very rich soil as the taste is compromised.

I always let some plants go to seed so I can save the seed for next year. Bees and beneficial insects love the flowers. Once you can see

Sow your coriander seeds directly in the garden around and under larger plants. I give my coriander protection from the harsh sun by growing it under large-leaved courgette plants.

In summer your coriander may bolt to seed. If it does, collect the seeds for next season. The flowers will encourage beneficial insects into your garden.

seeds forming at the top of the plant, snip off the stems, place the stems in a paper bag and hang in a cool dry place. The seeds will fall to the bottom of the bag when dry.

Uses

- You can add the ground seeds to breads or cakes, or use to flavour fish and poultry.

- Ground coriander seeds can be used as a dusting powder to repel many types of insects, especially aphids.

- Plant coriander around carrot seedlings as a deterrent to the carrot fly pest.

DILL

Dill is a tall lanky herb. It grows to about one metre in height. It looks like fennel, with similar feathery leaves.

Dill prefers rich soil. Add plenty of compost to improve the soil's water-holding capacity. Plant in full sun and protect from wind.

Dill can be planted any time of the year except winter. It is best to sow it directly from seed, as it does not transplant well. You can start harvesting the leaves within two months of planting.

The yellow flowerheads will attract beneficial insects and bees. Dill will deter white cabbage butterfly and mites. Grow it with your brassicas. It is also a good companion to lettuce, onions and cabbage.

Uses

- Serve dill leaves with fish, and in salads.

- Use the seeds in pickles and vinegars, or in herbal teas to aid digestion.

TOP TIP

Throw a handful of herbs in the bottom of your rubbish bin to keep it smelling nice.

Each dill flower is made up of many tiny single flowers. Its umbrella shape provides an easy landing platform for insects. The seeds can be used in cooking.

MINT

Mint is a hardy impossible-to-kill herb. There are no excuses – not even for the most brown-fingered gardener – for not growing some. A word of warning: unless you want mint rampaging through your garden, always grow this herb in a pot or bucket sunk into the soil. This stops runaway plants popping up all over your garden.

Sunken pot planting

This method stops suckers taking root and the plant spreading.

Materials

- 1 terracotta (frost-proof) or plastic pot at least 30 cm in diameter, with drainage holes
- good-quality potting mix
- mint plant

Method

- Dig a hole slightly larger than the diameter of the pot, in the area of the garden you wish to grow your mint.
- Place the pot in the hole, with the top of the pot level with the soil surface.
- Place some stones in base of the pot over the drainage holes.
- Fill the pot with potting mix, and plant the mint.
- Backfill around the pot with garden soil.

Mint prefers a moist semi-shaded area – but it is so tenacious it will grow anywhere.

There are many varieties of mint with different flavours, such as apple or spearmint. Pick the leaves when they are young and tender. Pick the tips regularly to keep the plant compact.

Uses

Where would our New Zealand lamb be without mint sauce? Mint also makes a lovely addition to massage oil.

Homemade mint sauce

- 1 handful freshly picked mint leaves
- 2 cups malt vinegar
- 2 tbs raw sugar

Mix the ingredients in microwave-proof bowl. Warm in microwave for 1–2 minutes.

Massage oil or rich body oil

Place a handful of mint leaves (peppermint or pennyroyal is best) in a glass jar with a lid. Pour 500 ml of unscented oil (e.g. sunflower, almond or baby oil) over leaves. Place jar in sun and shake several times a day. Ready to use after three weeks.

Mix the ingredients in microwave-proof bowl. Warm in microwave for 1–2 minutes.

MARJORAM AND OREGANO

These two herbs are very closely related. They both like well-drained, warm and sunny positions. If your garden experiences winter frosts, grow oregano, as this is frost tolerant. These plants both make good ground covers as they are fast growing. You can propagate by root cuttings or dividing large clumps in winter.

TOP TIP

Soak willow sticks in water, and use the water to dip cuttings in prior to planting. The chemicals in willow aid growth.

Uses

- I interchange these herbs in recipes with no effect on the desired flavours. Use them in casseroles (add just before serving), sauces, stuffings, egg and cheese dishes, or in fruit salads.

- A small cotton bag or pillowslip stuffed with oregano and marjoram can aid sleep, while a hot bath infused with some freshly picked sprigs can help combat tiredness.

Marjoram flowering in summer.

PARSLEY

Parsley is very handy to have growing in the garden. I mostly grow the flat-leaved (Italian) parsley, and always let some plants self-seed, so I have a continuous supply of fresh leaves.

As with most herbs, the young leaves have the best taste. Parsley prefers constant moisture and sun. If you are planting seeds, soak them overnight in warm water to hasten germination. Pour boiling water along the prepared ground to warm the soil, and add moisture just prior to sowing the seeds. Parsley seed should only be kept for a year before sowing – old seed will not germinate. After a few years of letting some plants self-seed, you will have numerous plants popping up throughout the garden.

Uses

- Parsley makes a great garnish or addition to salads.

- I feed excess seeds to my chickens as a natural wormer and tonic.

- Parsley is a great remedy for bad breath – the morning after a meal at the local Thai restaurant, munch on a handful of parsley to make yourself more kissable.

If you are short on space, underplant trees in tubs with herbs. The feijoa in this wine barrel is underplanted with parsley and chives.

ROSEMARY

Rosemary is as tough as old boots. There are rosemary plants growing out of cracks in our concrete drive.

Rosemary likes full sun and good drainage, and thrives in poor soil. There are varieties that grow as ground covers, or varieties that grow in an upright form. Both have deep blue flowers in summer that are loved by bees.

If your rosemary bush starts to yellow it may be getting too much water or nitrogen-rich fertiliser. Best growing results come from treating rosemary mean.

The upright varieties make great hedges, and can create a formal look if clipped regularly. Keep the trimmings to throw on the barbecue for flavour and aroma.

The easiest way to propagate rosemary is to take semi-hardwood cuttings any time during the year. Place the cuttings in a sandy soil mix, and within six weeks most will have developed roots and be growing vigorously. This is a very cheap way to grow your own hedge!

TOP TIP

To kill bacteria and speed up root growth, dip fresh cuttings in unheated honey before planting.

Uses

- In cooking: lamb cooked with rosemary is delicious. (Note: rosemary has a strong taste so be careful not to overdo its application in the kitchen.)

- Use firm rosemary twigs as skewers for barbecuing meat.

- Put rosemary sprigs in dog kennels and in chickens' laying boxes to keep lice and fleas away.

Bees love rosemary flowers. Regular picking of the growth tips will keep your bush compact.

SAGE

Sage is another Mediterranean herb that prefers a hot sunny position with free-draining soil. It is frost and heat tolerant. There are many species of sage, and most are long-lived and tough. You can grow them easily from seed as long as you keep the seed moist until it has germinated. You can also propagate by layering: fix a branch onto the soil with a metal peg, or hold down with a small stone, and cover the area with soil. New roots will form and then you can snip off the branch from the parent plant and transplant.

I grow the purple sage as I find it so ornamental. I always let it flower, as the bees love it.

Uses

Use sage leaves to stuff poultry, or fry the leaves and add to pasta dishes.

Purple sage growing with orange calendula. I love sage leaves on my pizzas. The cooked leaves are crunchy and yummy.

THYME

Thyme is a small-leaved, low-growing, creeping plant. When you rub the leaves it is intensely aromatic. Thyme produces tiny pink or white flowers in summer. Bees love thyme flowers, and use them to make a strong tasty honey.

Thyme produces its best flavour when the plant is in flower. Again it is a perfect herb to have in the garden, as it thrives on neglect. Don't overwater, don't fertilise – just ignore it and it will reward you with lots of leaves. (I love those sorts of plants.)

Thyme grows from cuttings or seeds. Take cuttings from the mature twiggy branches, place them in a pot full of sand and keep moist. It is best to take these cuttings when the plant is not in flower.

You can sow thyme seed in spring when the soil temperature has warmed to above 15°C. The seed is small, so just sprinkle some sand over it.

If you have a small lawn or an area of lawn that is hard to mow, maybe under or around your clothesline, consider growing a thyme lawn. Plant different varieties for a checkerboard effect. The thyme will soon spread and create a mow-free lawn. These sorts of lawns can take a little bit of foot traffic and be none the worse for wear. The added bonus is the aromatic fragrance they release when trodden on.

Uses

• Place little bunches of thyme in your linen cupboard between sheets. Not only does it make the sheets smell nice, but it also helps keep moths and other creepy crawlies out of your cupboards.

• Use as a disinfectant: see Top Tip below.

TOP TIP

Simmer the leaves of rosemary, thyme, sage and lavender in 1 litre of water for 45 minutes. Cool, strain and place in a spray bottle. Use as a natural disinfectant around the home. Will keep for one week in the fridge.

TARRAGON

This herb is great cooked with chicken, eggs and potatoes. In gourmet circles it is thought of as the ultimate luxury herb. It is very important to buy and grow French tarragon, not its inferior cousin Russian tarragon. If your tarragon bush is growing like a rampant weed you have a Ruski in your garden! If it is neat, tidy and well behaved, you have the French variety.

A good French tarragon leaf should almost numb your tongue when you chew on it. Anything inferior will taste like you are chewing cud.

Tarragon likes fertile soil and full sun. It prefers its own personal space, so don't crowd it with other herbs. It grows best in a cooler spot in the garden and will die down in winter. Regular picking of the growing tips keeps the plant bushy. It is best grown from cuttings or by dividing the root.

French tarragon won't take over your herb garden, as Russian tarragon is inclined to do.

MAKE A HERB SPIRAL: A STEP-BY-STEP GUIDE

A herb spiral is a great way of growing a lot of herbs in a confined space. Thanks to its shape and design, the herb spiral also creates microclimates for the herbs' particular growing requirements.

A herb spiral is easy to water, maintain and harvest. You can make your herb spiral to whatever dimensions you wish, but I find that about one metre in diameter is best. Any bigger and it becomes too difficult to reach in to harvest the herbs.

The location of your herb spiral is important. Choose a position that is close to your kitchen and outside tap, and receives all-day sun. If you position your herb spiral at the bottom of the garden, your herbs will probably never be used.

Step 1: Materials

You will need:

• rocks, bricks, or similar, for creating spiralled edging

• compost

• herbs to plant

• garden soil.

Step 2: Make a round mound

Mound up some garden soil until it is around half a metre in height by about one metre in diameter. Compact the mound with your feet or the back of a spade. If you have any concrete rubble or stones to dispose of, use them as a base and then cover with soil.

Step 3: Make a spiral

Following a spiral pattern, create an edge up around the mound using the rocks. Use the largest rocks around the base and spiral them up to the top as they get smaller. As you wind up the spiral with the rocks, fill in any gaps with smaller gravel or stones. Fill any hollows or gaps with compost. I find it best to overfill with the compost, compact it as much as you can and then wet it thoroughly with a hose.

Step 4: Plant the herbs

The herb spiral creates a variety of niches for your herbs. Plant herbs that love hot dry conditions on the top and the northern side. Herbs that require some shade are best planted on the southern side. Herbs that need moisture do best when planted around the base of the spiral (the dampest area).

A herb spiral is a great space saver and creates lots of nooks and crannies for all your herbs.

PREFERRED CONDITIONS FOR TYPES OF HERBS

Dryest	Dry	Medium	Wet	Shade
Thyme	Oregano	Basil	Vietnamese mint	Mint
Sage	Marjoram	Coriander	Watercress	Lemon balm
Rosemary	Lemon grass	Parsley		Rocket
Aloe		Chives		Coriander (in summer)
Lavender		Borage		
		Bergamot		

TOP TIP

Plant chamomile around any struggling plants. It will give them a boost and encourage strong growth. Use the flowers for a relaxing bath.

Make your own herb markers by collecting and painting flat river stones.

When good mint goes BAD! One mint plant has taken over this garden. To get rid of it you need to pull out every piece of underground runner. Avoid this in your garden by planting mint in a pot.

CHAPTER SIX

GROWING FLOWERS

EVEN IN AN EDIBLE GARDEN IT IS STILL NICE TO HAVE SOME COLOUR AND PRETTINESS, AND FLOWERS ARE A GREAT WAY TO PROVIDE THIS. CUT FLOWERS CAN ALSO PROVIDE YOU WITH A BIT OF EXTRA CASH TO PAY FOR THAT NEXT ORDER OF SEEDS OR FRUIT TREES. WHY NOT SEE IF YOU CAN SELL SOME OF YOUR FLOWERS TO LOCAL BUSINESSES? HAIR SALONS, CAFÉS, BANKS AND TRAVEL AGENTS ALWAYS NEED FRESH FLOWERS FOR THEIR COUNTER DISPLAYS. YOU COULD ALSO SET UP A SMALL STAND AT YOUR GATE WITH AN HONESTY BOX TO SELL THE EXCESS – EVERYONE ENJOYS HAVING FRESH FLOWERS IN THEIR HOUSE. THE KIDS CAN EARN SOME MONEY BY MANNING THE STAND DURING THE HOLIDAYS.

Hydrangeas add colour and beauty in the garden.

Make some extra cash by selling homegrown flowers at your gate.

CARE OF CUT FLOWERS

To make your precious flowers last for as long as possible, follow these simple steps.

- Pick flowers in the early morning, and have a bucket full of fresh water with you to place flowers in as soon as they are cut.

- Use a sharp knife or scissors to cut the stems.

- Choose flowers that are just starting to open.

- Always remove the lower leaves from the stem, as decaying leaves will contaminate the water and shorten the life of your flowers.

- Change the vase water every day, and re-cut stems on a diagonal. Always cut the stems under warm running water. The stems will immediately draw up water rather than air.

- Don't jam your vase with too many flowers. Flowers last longer with some air circulation.

- Place the vase in a position out of direct sunlight.

- Place an aspirin and a dash of bleach in the water. The aspirin changes the acidity of the water, making it easier for water to draw up into the stem, and the bleach stops fungi and bacteria growing. If I have some lemonade I also add around half a cup to the vase water as a cheap alternative to commercial cut flower food.

TOP TIP

To help keep flowers upright in a vase, crisscross transparent tape over the top of the vase and insert flowers through the openings.

Pick your flowers in the early morning using sharp scissors. Choose flowers that are just starting to open.

Brighten up any room with a vase of homegrown cut flowers. A bunch this size would cost over $10 at the florist. Grow them for free in your garden.

TOP FLOWERS TO GROW IN YOUR GARDEN

The following flowers are ones I have had success growing. Many of them are beneficial to the garden – for attracting bees and other pollinators, providing a food source for beneficial insects, or returning nitrogen or carbon to the soil.

SUNFLOWERS

Summer just isn't summer without big yellow sunflower faces grinning down at you. Plant them from the middle of spring right through to the middle of summer. You can plant the seeds directly into the garden to save time, but you will find that the birds eat at least some of them.

Sunflowers make an excellent cut flower – they will last for up to a week.

Use tin cans or takeaway coffee cups (see page 50) to protect the seeds and emerging seedlings from feathered thieves. Alternatively, sow seed in trays and plant out when around 10 cm tall.

Sunflowers prefer fertile, free-draining soil in full sun. (Fertile soil is dark in colour, moist, and when you dig it over you see lots of earthworms.)

Each sunflower has a personality of its own, and I love the way their faces track the sun across the garden. Kids seem to love them, too. There are many varieties, from dwarf to the towering skyscraper varieties that grow up to nearly four metres tall. Over the years I have grown many types that have cross-pollinated and now give me my own particular bouquet. You can buy seeds of many types from the garden centre, or, if you don't mind the budget version, go to the pet shop and buy a packet meant for parrots. Fling handfuls around the garden and you will have smiley faces staring at you all summer, and plenty of excess to sell.

In my vegetable garden I grow climbing beans up and around the stem of each sunflower, using the stalk as a living support for the beans. Once the beans and sunflowers have finished for the season, I chop them down and leave both to rot back into the soil. The beans return nitrogen to the soil and the sunflowers return important carbon.

Apparently some people think sunflowers inhibit the growth of surrounding plants, but I have never witnessed this – in fact I find the tall varieties shade the soil, protecting lettuce, coriander, silver beet and brassicas from the hot summer sun.

Bees love sunflowers, as do chickens – I save some flowerheads to feed to my chickens as a treat.

BLACK-EYED SUSAN

This sturdy, hardy and striking plant looks great mass planted in any perennial border. It is a prairie plant from North America, and produces a profusion of yellow daisy-like flowers with a black cone centre. These make excellent cut flowers and are long-lasting. The plant prefers a sunny spot with friable (crumbly) moist soil. Butterflies and bees love the flowers.

In late autumn the petals fall away leaving the dried cone, which can be used in dried arrangements. I leave the dried flower stalk in the garden as it gives interest throughout winter as a giant outside dried bouquet. Come spring I cut it down to add to the compost heap and the plant bursts into life again.

You can buy black-eyed Susan at most garden centres. Increase your stock by dividing the root after a few years.

Black-eyed Susan creates a sea of yellow in your garden. Plant it to attract butterflies and bees, and have cut flowers for your home.

PURPLE CONEFLOWER

This is another North American prairie plant. It likes full sun and well-drained soil. It is drought tolerant, heat tolerant, and does not like any fertiliser – a perfect plant on so many levels! Purple coneflower has deep green, serrated-edged leaves and fabulous broad purple petals that hang down from the central cone. They look stunning mass planted in the garden, and bring in the bees and butterflies in their masses. As a cut flower, the stalk remains rigid and it lasts for at least five days in a vase. As with black-eyed Susan, the dried round black cones make a great dried arrangement.

The purple coneflower.

SWEET PEAS

Sweet peas are fun and easy to grow. Bunches of these pretty flowers will fill a room with their lovely fragrance. Plant from seed, or as seedlings from the garden centre, in spring. The roots like a cool area. They require a structure for suppor; for example, grow them up a trellis, bamboo tepee or tree, down rock walls, or let them spill out of hanging baskets. They like an alkaline soil, so apply some garden lime prior to planting. Provide plenty of water and pick flowers regularly to encourage more blooms. As the plant is a legume and fixes nitrogen, dig the old plants back into the soil to replenish.

Sweet peas come in many shades.

HYDRANGEAS

Not so long ago hydrangeas were considered a real granny's flower, but thanks to a retro revival they are once again very trendy. Apparently they are very popular in France – and let's face it, those French know a thing or two about fashion.

Hydrangeas are a perfect plant for that dappled shady area where nothing else wants to grow. All they need is some water in summer. Big drifts of hydrangeas are a great way to have an easy-care garden with a stunning floral display. As a cut flower they are superb and last for a long time. Cut the flower and soak the stems in deep cold water for one hour. The blooms will last for several weeks in a vase.

When planting hydrangeas, add compost and work this in well to get them off to a great start. They can handle a little sun, but the flowers last longer and are a better colour if the plant has shade. The flower colour is influenced by soil conditions. Blues are intensified by acid conditions (pH4.5–5.5) and pinks, whites and red by alkaline conditions (pH6–7). If you want to enhance these colours, add garden lime to the red, whites and pinks, and ammonium sulphate or aluminium sulphate to the blue ones.

Prune the bush in late autumn. Reduce its size by half, cutting to just above a pair of nodes. (The nodes are the junctions where the leaves grow from the stem.) This will promote good flowering next season.

A hydrangea bush in early summer. Each round globe of hydrangea is made up of many smaller flowers.

TOP TIP

For strong-smelling flowers such as daisies and marigolds, add a pinch of bicarbonate of soda to the vase water. This causes them to give off less odour.

GLOBE THISTLE

This plant is part of the thistle family, but don't let that put you off. In fact why not plant it under a window to discourage burglars! The globe thistle plant is very low maintenance, and will flower from early summer to autumn. The flowers are bright blue when new, fading to a steely blue. They are perfectly round, and about the size of a golf ball. The bees and butterflies love them.

Globe thistle flowers make a real statement in any modern garden.

They are wonderful as a cut flower, and if you put them in a vase without any water they will slowly fade to a steely grey. They'd look fabulous as a centrepiece in a minimalist, modern house, or as an arrangement in a trendy inner-city café or bistro.

This plant likes well-drained and sandy soil. It grows to around 1.2 metres, so is great for the back of a border. When it is not in flower, the plant looks like a thistle, so make sure you don't pull it out by accident in a weeding frenzy, as has happened on occasion in my garden. It is best to plant globe thistles as seeds – you can't divide them, like most perennials, as they have a long taproot. They can sometimes be found in the perennial section at your garden centre, or obtain by mail order from nurseries.

BISHOP'S FLOWER

I grow this plant in and around my vegetable garden, as it is great for attracting all those 'good guy' insects. It is also very attractive, with white lacy flowers growing in an umbrella shape. It makes an excellent cut flower, creating a similar effect to gypsophila, but it is much easier to grow.

I plant as seeds, either just sprinkled around or incorporated in seed bombs (see page 169). The plant requires around one square metre of space and grows to around 200 cm high. Plant in full sun or semi shade in fertile well-drained soil. It will flower from spring to late summer. It is an annual, so collect some seeds in autumn to replant in spring.

Bishop's flower: an alternative to gypsophila, and much easier to grow. You'll find ladybirds in most flowerheads, enjoying the nectar.

LIATRIS PURPLE TORCH

If you enjoy butterflies in your garden, this is a great plant to grow. It is in hot demand with florists, and looks stunning with its vertical, sword-like, purple (or white) flowers that grow to around 40 cm long. The flowers open from the top down, giving them a tufted appearance. It creates a great vertical accent in the garden, if you can see it through the butterflies!

Plant in full sun to semi shade in moist well-drained soil. When established it is drought tolerant and tough as old boots.

You can buy seeds from mail-order nurseries, or established plants in the perennial sections of many garden centres.

The purple spikes of the Liatris flower.

Peonies come in many different colours.

PEONIES

If you live in a climate where you can grow these beautiful flowers, then do so – they are dead easy and will reward you with gorgeous flowers from October through to December. Cut stems sell for $5 in most flower shops; need I say more?

Peonies need cold, frosty winters and hot summers. They don't like humidity. They do best in compost-rich soil that won't dry out in summer, in full sun. Each plant can grow to a metre round, so when planting make sure you give each one room to develop as they don't like to be crowded.

There are many varieties of peonies, from single to double with frilly petals, ranging in colour from white, through pink, red and yellow. You can buy dormant root divisions from garden centres and specialist nurseries in autumn and winter. Plant with about five centimetres of compost or well-rotted manure. They love potash, so I spread the ash from our fire around mine. Peonies are disease free, and insects don't seem to find them very tasty, so once established they are the perfect self-care plant.

Peonies can be expensive to buy; growing your own is much cheaper.

Cut peonies before they bloom, they last a lot longer. When they have finished their magnificent display, throw them in your compost to recycle.

CHAPTER SEVEN

COMPOSTING

A COMPOST HEAP IS A PILE OF LOVELY ROTTING ORGANIC MATTER THAT FEEDS YOUR SOIL, THUS FEEDING YOUR PLANTS AND EVENTUALLY YOU. A GOOD COMPOST PILE CAN TURN RUBBISH INTO RICH COMPOST IN AROUND FOUR WEEKS. A BAD ONE WILL SIT AROUND BREEDING FLIES AND HIDING RATS FOR YEARS!

Many people think a compost pile has to look like this: unsightly and taking up a large area. But there are other ways to create compost that require little space and avoid smells, flies and an untidy heap.

It makes good sense to make your own compost:

- it makes your plants grow bigger and tastier.
- it turns rubbish into plant food instead of having to pay to have it taken away.
- it encourages earthworms and healthy microorganisms into your garden, and
- you save money by not having to buy compost, fertiliser and disease-controlling sprays.

Most importantly, you can't have a vegetable garden without making compost. Growing great vegetables all starts with growing great soil, and that starts with growing great compost.

Sites of all sizes can be composted. If you don't have a dedicated composting area, you can make small batches of compost next to the vegetable beds: use a cylinder of chicken wire, or just create a straight-sided pile. Alternatively, dig a trench and bury any kitchen waste directly into the garden.

Consider making your own compost tumbler (see page 118), which will give you rich compost in just four weeks.

If you keep hens you can compost in situ by throwing all kitchen scraps, lawn clippings and other organic waste into their run. They will scratch about, eat what they like and turn the rest, over time, into rich organic compost.

HOW TO MAKE GREAT COMPOST

Making good compost is a little like making good bread. It is important to have the right ingredients and to mix them the right way. Carbon organic matter is like the flour; nitrogen organic matter is like the sugar; and the microorganisms and fungi that start the process of decomposition are like the yeast. Just like bread, compost needs air and moisture and requires kneading, in the form of turning and mixing, either manually or by other means. And like a freshly baked loaf of bread, a well-rotted compost pile will smell warm and sweet – though I wouldn't suggest you slice it up and eat it!

Perfect compost ingredients! I call this my flotsam and jetsam. It is the end result after sweeping the drive: small sticks, leaves, dust, small stones and dirt.

TOP TIP

Shared by Julie, Green Community Forum

Save pieces of brown paper, paper bags etc., and use them to line your kitchen scraps bin (or use newspaper if the ink is compost friendly). The paper goes into the compost with the scraps, and there's no slimy goo left in your bin.

WHAT CAN YOU COMPOST?

Basically you can add anything that was once living to your compost, including:

- coffee grounds
- tea bags
- newspaper
- full vacuum cleaner bags
- shredded cotton clothing
- hessian sacks
- pine needles
- seaweed
- nut shells and hulls
- untreated sawdust
- human and animal hair
- feather, fur and wool
- wood ashes
- leaves, lawn clippings, hedge trimmings and weeds.

Don't try to compost these:

- pig, dog, cat or human manure – they will just encourage flies and can spread disease

- plastic (unless you're happy to wait for at least 500 years)

- big bones – bury these under trees instead; they will slowly rot down, replacing vital nutrients

- fat, oil, salt, borax, herbicides, pesticides: all these will kill the good microorganisms

- weed seeds, unless you are sure your compost will heat up to above 50°C (see page 112)

- meat, unless you are happy with rodents playing tag around your compost all day and night

- thick layers of grass clippings, or anything that might clog together – mix them up with other stuff and they will be fine.

TWO MAGIC INGREDIENTS FOR THE COMPOST

If you are serious about composting (and if you want to grow great veggies you will be), there are two vital compost ingredients you need to grow in your garden.

Russian comfrey

Comfrey is an herbaceous perennial. You can buy it in the herb section at most garden centres. It's full title is *Symphytum x uplandicum*, variety Bocking 14.

Comfrey is a particularly valuable source of fertility to the organic gardener. It is easy to grow, and its leaves can be cut several times a year.

The plant develops a long taproot that mines minerals up to the surface and into its large leaves. The leaves are therefore rich in vital minerals, particularly nitrogen and potassium. Potassium is especially important for flower, seed and fruit production. The leaves decay quickly so can be used in the compost as an activator. Use only wilted leaves in the compost to prevent any new plants sprouting.

Bocking 14 variety does not set seed so will not self-seed, but any small piece of root will grow, so think carefully about where you want to plant it as it will be there for ever. (See page 114 for more on comfrey.)

Yarrow (Achillea)

Yarrow leaves will also activate the compost – just a handful will get it going. As the leaves rot they will release nitrogen and potassium into the organic matter.

Yarrow also produces an attractive flower that will attract beneficial insects into the garden.

Yarrow (Achillea) is a useful and attractive plant to have in the garden. It comes in shades of red, yellow and pink.

COMPOSTING TECHNIQUES

You don't need a compost bin to make compost; in fact most of the ones you can buy are really lousy at making compost – they just make a pile look tidy.

The five following techniques are different ways to create compost. You may find only one is suited to your situation, or you may use them all during different times of the year. None requires expensive bins or additives, just lots of organic matter.

CLASSIC COMPOSTING

Start collecting the materials for a classic compost heap well in advance, so that you can make everything in one go. As well as the organic materials you will also need either stakes, downpipes, or bunches of bamboo or dried corn stalks (to create airshafts), and materials to help you shape the sides (e.g. old wooden pallets or real estate signs).

Drive the stakes into the soil, aiming for an area at least one metre square. Lightly fork over the existing soil to help microorganisms activate the compost. Place coarse twigs or branches as a base, and then start layering with alternating hand width (about 10 cm) layers of green (nitrogen-rich) matter and brown (carbon-rich) matter. Sprinkle each new layer with water, and add animal manure, blood and bone or wilted comfrey leaves.

Make the pile all in one go. Try to build it with straight sides, at least one metre high. Then remove the stakes and cover the heap with a tarpaulin or some soil.

Check the heap in two weeks. If it is dry, sprinkle more water through it. Reach into the middle of the pile – it should be very hot. If it is not, remix the ingredients with a pitchfork, adding more manure or grass clippings. If you require compost fast, turn the heap every week. If you are lazy, like me, let nature take its course and leave compost for three to five months. By then you should have produced lovely rich, dark compost for your garden.

A good trick is to make your compost pile right next to, or actually in, your vegetable garden. When the compost has matured you only need to push it over and you have an instant garden. No wheelbarrow necessary.

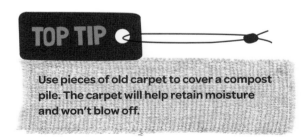

TOP TIP

Use pieces of old carpet to cover a compost pile. The carpet will help retain moisture and won't blow off.

CRATER COMPOSTING

A compost crater is a hole in the ground filled with layers of organic matter, which is then left to work its magic and turn everything into rich compost without any need for you to mix or turn the heap.

This method is great if you intend to plant trees in the near future. The downside is that it requires some digging – no problem if you enjoy a bit of spadework or are lucky enough to have someone burly in the household!

Dig a hole in the ground about one metre square. (I make mine slightly smaller as I'm always afraid of losing a small child!) Drive a thick stake or length of downpiping into the base of the crater. Place branches or thick plant stalks at the base and then start layering compost materials about a hand width thick. Alternate green materials (nitrogen rich) such as lawn clippings, hedge trimmings or weeds, with brown materials (carbon rich) such as straw, leaves, pine needles or sawdust. Sprinkle water on each layer. Sprinkle some manure, blood and bone or wilted comfrey leaves as you build up the layers, to activate the compost. Cover with topsoil. After two weeks remove the stake or piping, to aid ventilation.

After four weeks the pile will have subsided, so add some more topsoil or plant your tree or shrub.

SUPER-SPEEDY COMPOST

Collect the ingredients for your compost and lay them on the lawn. Shred the ingredients by mowing them with a lawn mower. Spread a large tarpaulin or piece of black plastic on the lawn, and pile the material on it as widely as you can. Wet the pile with a liquid compost tea (see page 116). Cover the pile with another tarpaulin or large piece of plastic.

Turn the pile every three days by rolling the tarpaulin, and re-wetting the heap with compost tea each time. Within two weeks you will have rich compost.

The secret to this method is the combination of frequent turning, finely shredded matter and the high nitrogen level.

If you want to avoid the laborious turning, place the shredded material into a large plastic drum with a fitted lid and some small holes drilled along the sides. (Find these large 200-litre drums at recyclers.) The holes allow air exchange within the compost. Put the drum on its side and roll it around the garden every day.

DEEP LITTER COMPOST USING CHICKENS

If you keep chickens, this is an easy way to make compost. It allows you to take advantage of the chickens' natural characteristic of scratching and pecking through organic matter.

Throw all your weeds, leaves, kitchen scraps, sawdust, coffee grounds, straw and prunings into the chicken run. The chickens will scratch through it, eating what they want, pooping in it, and constantly turning it over. Each year you can barrow out loads of nitrogen-rich compost and then start the process again.

Chicken droppings are very rich in nitrogen – great for composting. The heavier breeds, such as Light Sussex, Barnevelder, Orpington or Plymouth Rocks, are best for this and the secret is to throw lots of dry straw between other materials. The straw really gets the chickens scratching and mixing.

Chickens are great composters, turning organic matter into rich and fertile compost. Trying situating your chicken run under fruit trees – the trees provide them with shade, whilst the chickens feed the rootzone and eat any fallen fruit.

COMPOST IN A BAG

Even if you live in an apartment you can make compost for your pot plants from recycled kitchen waste. You will need a medium-sized bag and a twist tie. Place five cups of shredded kitchen scraps in the bag – this could be coffee grounds, tea bags, fruit peelings, vegetable peelings, shredded paper, hair from your brush or anything else you can find. Add one cup of garden soil to the bag. This is important, as it provides the all-important microorganisms to kick-start the process. Pour in one cup of warm water and seal the bag. Squeeze and roll the bag to mix the contents. Every second day, open the bag so that air can be exchanged. Keep the mixture moist but not wet. In four to six weeks you should have rich homemade compost to feed to your pot plants.

TROUBLE SHOOTING

Forty-eight hours after making your compost, your pile should have heated up to around 55°C, which is the temperature of hot water from a tap. If you put your hand into the middle of the pile it should therefore feel really hot. If your compost pile has failed to heat up in this time, pull it apart and build it again. Failure to heat up means that the necessary microorganisms have scorned your carefully made home or diet.

Ask yourself these questions:

- Is the pile too wet? Squeeze a handful of the mixture – no drops of moisture should fall.

- Is the pile too dry? It should feel damp, like a squeezed sponge.

- Has it been compacted, preventing air from reaching inside?

- Are there too many bulky ingredients? All the material should be mulched or chopped prior to adding to the pile. Aim at having each individual piece of material no bigger than a cake of soap.

- Is the pile too small? It needs to be at least one metre square for the centre to heat up.

- Too few nitrogen-rich ingredients (green stuff) is like offering the microbes stale bread rather than chocolate cake. Add fresh grass clippings to kick-start the decomposition process.

- Are the layers too thick? Lots of thin layers (about 10 cm deep) is the key.

There are no deep dark secrets about composting. Composting is easy, fun, and something we all should do, no matter how small our properties are. The rewards in plant health and growth and the increased health of your soil are quick to be seen, not to mention the benefit to our planet from the reduction of waste going to landfill.

GROW YOUR OWN COMPOST: GREEN MANURE CROP

Growing your own green manure crop is not about cultivating some sort of cow patty bush, you'll be relieved to know (though I have to admit I wouldn't mind one of those in my garden!). Growing green manure crops is a lazy way of composting, involving no heavy turning or loading wheelbarrows. Just grow it and cut it to replenish and feed the soil.

The technique involves growing certain crops in your vegetable garden, then cutting them off at their ankles and leaving them to rot down, feeding your soil with important nutrients. Instead of leaving vegetable garden space empty (fallow), plant these crops in late summer and allow them to grow over winter. Cut them down in early spring and let them rot on top of the soil for three to four weeks before digging over the soil and sowing your spring crops.

A winter green manure crop also acts as a living mulch, and reduces the loss of soil when it's windy or during heavy rain.

The easiest and most cost-effective way of growing these crops is by seed. Most garden centres sell bulk packets of green manure crop seeds. After you have harvested your late summer crops, smooth over the soil with a rake and sow the seeds according to the instructions on the packet. Then lightly rake again to cover the seeds. Each crop will have different growing rates and harvesting times. When the plants start to develop flowers it is time to cut them down and dig them back into the soil. It is as simple as that. (If you let them set seed you may get a 'weed' problem.)

The following is a list of crops that I use as green manures.

PHACELIA

This is probably my best pick, as it has so many other benefits. The vibrant flowers attract beneficial insects such as hoverflies, bees and lacewings, and look nice in the garden. Phacelia does self-seed, but it is not invasive, so I let it come up wherever it wants – if I need that space I just pull it out and use it as a mulch around vegetable plants.

Tender young mustard seedlings are great in salads and sandwiches. The chickens love them too. Any not eaten by family or chickens is used as a green manure crop.

Easy to grow and loved by beneficial insects, phacelia makes a great green manure crop.

MUSTARD SEED

Sow this thickly. (You can use the small seedlings in your salads or sandwiches.) Dig the mustard in when it's about 20 cm high. The flowers are an attractive yellow colour – if you let a few plants flower they will attract bees and bumblebees into your garden.

LUPINS

These are great nitrogen fixers: nitrogen from the atmosphere is harnessed by the roots and stored as small white nodules on the roots. When the lupins' roots rot, the nitrogen becomes available for your plants to reuse.

BROAD BEANS AND PEAS

When your harvest of broad beans and peas is over, chop the stalks into pieces about 10–20 cm long with a sharp handsaw or knife, and then let them rot where they were grown. This will replace all the nitrogen back into the soil. You can follow them with a nitrogen-hungry crop such as brassica. (As a general rule, nitrogen-hungry crops are those that produce lots of leafy growth, such as broccoli, cauliflower, silver beet and spinach.)

Broad bean stalks are slow to rot. In the meantime, as they lie on the garden, they are useful for protecting small seedlings from birds. A great plant doing two jobs at once.

OATS

These provide a fast-growing cover, and break down quickly when ploughed back into the soil.

CORN AND SUNFLOWERS

Not strictly green manure crops, these two plants are good for putting carbon back into the soil. Carbon holds the structure and nutrients of the soil together – without it, the soil structure eventually collapses. A lack of carbon was one of the causes of the Dust Bowl that occurred in the USA during the 1930s.

After growing these crops, cut their fibrous stalks into 10–20 cm lengths and dig them back into the soil. The stalks can take around six months to fully break down, but chopping them into pieces and keeping them covered with soil will hasten this process.

COMFREY, THE WONDER HERB

Comfrey has been used for centuries. It was known as 'Knitbone', and was used as a poultice to mend broken bones.

By growing comfrey in your garden you have an instant plant food, fertiliser and compost activator on hand at all times. Russian comfrey (*Symphytum x uplandicum*), Bocking 14 variety, has the same chemical makeup as compost (ten parts carbon to one part nitrogen) and is said to outperform farmyard manure and compost for feeding plants.

Comfrey is a perennial herb that dies down in winter and regrows in spring. Think carefully about where you want to grow your comfrey, as once planted it is there for good. Comfrey can also be grown in a large pot. The Bocking 14 variety is sterile so will not spread. You can propagate it by digging up a section of its root and cutting into three-centimetre segments. Replant these root sections horizontally and they will quickly establish into plants. For this very reason don't dig around the comfrey plants unless you want new plants sprouting everywhere –

Comfrey, ready to be harvested. The leaves are covered with fine hairs. When handling, wear gloves to avoid these hairs irritating your skin.

a fast way to get more plants is to put a rotary hoe through an established plant!

Comfrey grows vigorously, and you can cut and harvest the leaves many times over spring and summer. When using comfrey, make sure you cut only the leaf, not the stem, to reduce the risk of ending up with a garden full of comfrey.

Below are some great uses for comfrey.

- Wrap seed potatoes in wilted comfrey leaves before planting (see page 55).
- Throw good amounts of wilted comfrey leaves through your compost pile. The comfrey rots quickly, activating the composting process and heating the pile.
- Use comfrey to make fertiliser teas. Fill a hessian sack with comfrey leaves, farm manure, fish bones, seaweed and other organic matter, put the sack into a barrel and fill the barrel with water. After three weeks you'll have rich liquid fertiliser to give an instant boost to your plants. This is a natural

Before using comfrey in the garden, ensure it is wilted to prevent it from resprouting in your garden. Cut the leaves and lay them on concrete in the hot sun for several hours. The leaves should feel limp and have turned grey.

steroid – you can literally see your plants growing.

- Use cut comfrey leaves as a green mulch around fruit trees. As it rots it suppresses weeds and feeds the root zone with nutrients.
- Plant comfrey near your fruit trees – the flowers bring in the bees to help with pollination.
- Make your own compost potting mix by putting comfrey leaves and autumn leaves in a large wool or plastic sack. Sprinkle water and a handful of garden lime over the mixture and then leave in a cool place for three months. The mixture will rot down, producing beautiful rich compost.
- Use cut leaves as a green mulch around and under your growing vegetables.
- If you have a permanent chicken run, grow comfrey on the outside along the fence. The chickens will peck at the leaves through the wire but can't destroy the plant. Comfrey's medicinal properties are beneficial to chickens, and they love it.
- Plant comfrey along your boundary as a barrier to keep out couch and kikuyu grass.

Rotting comfrey leaves feed developing potatoes, helping to produce a bumper crop each year.

Grow comfrey in your urban orchard. It acts as a living weed mulch, attracts bees, and the cut leaves will feed your trees if left to rot around the root zone.

Rocket fuel for veggies. The top bucket is filled with bricks to compress the comfrey in the lower bucket. The 'black gold' drains through a hole into the plastic tray. Dilute by 10 times. (This brew does not produce a strong odour.)

- To make a hyper-charged liquid feed: drill a small hole in the base of a bucket, set the bucket on bricks and place a container under the hole to collect fluid. Fill the bucket with comfrey and then place a heavy weight, e.g. more bricks in a bucket, over the leaves (see photograph). Cover the bucket with a lid or a flat piece of wood. The comfrey will produce a black odourless fluid, which you can dilute by 10 times and spray onto the foliage of your vegetables.

See how it's done

Watch me explain how to grow and use comfrey around your garden at:
www.youtube.com/watch?v=Ou1Bh4Cr3s8

GARDEN TEAS:
MAKE YOUR OWN LIQUID FERTILISER

This tea has nothing to do with cucumber sandwiches and bone china tea sets. My version of garden tea is a lot smellier and far less refined! Forget about buying liquid fertiliser ever again – just follow these easy steps to brew your own.

A liquid fertiliser can be instantly absorbed by a plant when sprayed onto its leaves. Do this weekly as an instant boost to plant growth and to prevent disease. A handy tip is to spray in the early morning or evening when the plant's stomata are open, allowing the fertiliser to enter the plant. (Stomata is a fancy way of saying the plant's pores.)

You will need a large barrel with a fitted lid. Attach a plastic tap at the bottom to drain the liquid. (This is not imperative as you could just ladle the fluid out, but that makes for a very smelly job.) If you do have a tap, raise up the barrel, for example on bricks, so that you can place a bucket or watering can under the tap.

Get a hessian sack (you may be able to buy one cheaply from your local coffee roaster), or large onion bag, and fill with a quantity of any of the following ingredients. Don't worry about amounts or ratios – the secret is to use what you can find easily and to vary ingredients if you can:

- comfrey leaves
- animal manure
- seaweed
- homemade compost
- nettles
- coffee grounds
- garden weeds such as chickweed, dandelion, sow thistle, cleavers, fat hen and borage
- fish heads, crayfish bodies, kina (sea urchins)
- bones
- urine (luckily I have three young boys and a husband who are always looking for an excuse to 'go' outside – ask volunteers to be discreet!).

Place the filled sack into the barrel, fill the barrel with water and put on the lid. After three weeks the tea is ready to use. Pour it into a watering can and dilute with water so that it looks like weak tea. Water or spray on plants. Try to get as much as you can on the leaves. The 'tea' stinks, especially if you use comfrey, but the smell only lasts for about an hour.

Refill the barrel to get one more brew out of the ingredients. After you have used all of the second brew, spread the contents of the sack on the garden. If you have the materials and the space you can have several barrels at different stages of development, giving a constant supply for the garden.

Garden teas are easy to make in whatever qualities of ingredients you have access to. They are free and supply important minerals and nutrients for your plants. Give it a go – there's no excuse.

See how it's done

Watch me demonstrate how to make your own homemade organic liquid plant fertiliser at: http://www.youtube.com/watch?v=dEJiHHdjGeI

I make my compost tea in a large black plastic bin. A tap at the base makes it easy to drain off the brew.

MAKE A COMPOST TUMBLER: A STEP-BY-STEP GUIDE

A compost tumbler mixes and aerates organic material, producing compost in just four weeks. Compost tumblers are expensive to buy, but here is a simple way to make your own.

Step 1: Materials and tools

You will need:

- 1 large plastic food-grade drum (make sure it has been used to store food, not chemicals); look for them at plastic recyclers or demolition building yards

- 1 wooden board, or an old small stool, table or workbench

- 4 small castor wheels

- 2 hinges

- screws

- 1 Hasp and Staple galvanised latch, or other strong latch that will keep a hinged door fastened (if you are a skier, perhaps use one of your old ski boot buckles)

- jigsaw

- hand drill

- screwdriver.

Step 2: Cut out and fix the door

- Mark out a large square on the barrel as the position for the hinged door.

- Drill four holes, one at each corner of the square.

- Using the jigsaw, cut out the door.

- Screw the hinges to the door and then attach to the barrel with screws.

- Attach the latch on the opposite side to lock the door.

Step 3: Drill air holes

Drill holes about the size of a pencil every five centimetres around each end and the middle of the barrel. These holes help to aerate the mixture as it is being turned.

Step 4: Build a moveable stand

Fix the castor wheels onto the wooden board (or alternative stand).

Step 6: Wait for four weeks, then use

After four weeks your compost should be ready to use in the garden. Lift the drum onto the ground and roll it to wherever you need to put the compost. After using, leave about half a bucket of compost in the barrel as a starter for the next batch.

I only half fill the tumbler so it doesn't become too heavy to rotate.

See how it's done

Watch me demonstrate how to make and operate your own compost tumbler at: www.youtube.com/watch?v=a08WS-wDivl

Step 5: Fill and position the tumbler

Place the tumbler on its stand and fill with shredded organic matter such as paper, kitchen scraps, straw, garden weeds, coffee grounds and comfrey. This type of composting is not going to heat and destroy weed seeds, so avoid adding any seedheads and weed bulbs. Don't overfill the barrel – stop adding material when it is around half full or it becomes difficult to turn and does not aerate well. Dampen the mixture with a sprinkle of water from the hose. Put the tumbler in a sunny spot and rotate daily by manually turning whenever you walk past. The organic matter breaks down quickly thanks to this regular turning and aeration.

MAKE A HARVEST HIGH-RISE: A STEP-BY-STEP GUIDE

This contraption does four jobs at once. It makes rich compost, provides support for plants, provides warmth for plants and automatically feeds your plants. Better still, it follows the ideas of recycling and reusing in your garden.

A harvest high-rise can be used to grow peas, snow peas, cucumbers, eggplants, capsicums, runner beans, tomatoes or any other crop that requires some support during its growth.

Step 1: Materials and tools

You will need:

- 1 piece of PVC downpipe about 2 m long
- 1 length of reinforcing steel mesh or galvanised chicken wire (approx 4 m wide by 1.5 m high)
- 3 support stakes
- 1 plastic drink bottle
- 30 cm of tie wire or 4 cable ties
- cordless drill.

Step 2: Create a column

Using the steel mesh or chicken wire, make a column measuring about one metre in diameter. Secure with wire or cable ties, and put in a sunny position in the garden. Secure using the support stakes.

Step 3: Make some holes

Drill holes about the diameter of a pencil up and down the length of the pipe – around 20 holes in total.

Step 4: Put in the stopper and position the pipe

Jam the plastic drink bottle in one end of the pipe to act as a bung. Stand the pipe vertically in the middle of the wire column with the bottle at the bottom.

Step 5: Fill the harvest high-rise

Fill with layers of organic material, around the pipe, remembering to layer nitrogen-rich (green) material with carbon-rich (brown) material. Sprinkle water and add animal manure between the layers as you build up the compost to the top.

Step 6: Plant around the high-rise

Plant three to four plants (e.g. tomato plants) around the base of the column. As the plants grow, tie them to the wire for support. Water the plants through the pipe – the water will run through the compost, feeding the plants' roots with nutrients. The heat from the decomposition will keep the plants warm and protected from any late frosts. Any weeds can be thrown on top of the column to add to the compost.

Step 7: Empty the high-rise

When you have harvested your crop, tip over the column and use the rotted compost on the garden.

TOP TIP

Spray this mixture onto plants and soil to keep bugs and birds from nibbling your crops. It should also keep cats and dogs off your garden.

3 tablespoons Tabasco sauce

3 tablespoons wasabi sauce

500 ml water

a squirt of liquid soap.

CHAPTER EIGHT

MICRO – LIVESTOCK

THE TERM MICRO-LIVESTOCK REFERS TO SMALL SPECIES AND BREEDS OF ANIMAL, FROM BUGS, EARTHWORMS AND BEES UP TO SMALL BREEDS OF PIGS, GOATS AND SHEEP. IN THIS CHAPTER WE'LL LOOK AT THREE TYPES OF MICRO-LIVESTOCK THAT ARE A WONDERFUL ADDITION TO THE GREEN URBAN GARDEN: WORMS, CHICKENS AND BEES.

A bought worm farm houses layers of organic matter. The worms work their way through the layers, devouring everything and turning it into odour-free vermicasts. You can place these worm farms in garages, on patios, or even in cupboards.

WORM FARMING

Whether you live in the suburbs or in an apartment, worms are the perfect livestock for the urban gardener. These wonderfully low-maintenance pets don't need daily walks, scratch the sofa, require costly trips to the vet, or get the huff if you go on holiday.

Worms will chomp through all your vegetable scraps, vacuum cleaner bags, coffee grounds and even shredded envelopes and newspaper. They will reward you with buckets of black 'worm wees' to feed to your pot plants, and worm-made compost that you can use as a mulch around all your edible plants. 'Worm wees' is my magic potion – it will give any plant an instant growth boost. You can almost see the plants smile when you sprinkle it on them.

To make the best use of worms, set up a worm farm. You can keep it anywhere: in the garage, an unused corner of the garden, or even in a cupboard. When I told my long-suffering husband that I was getting 5000 new pets (and that he had to help me come up with names for each one), he didn't know whether to laugh or cry!

Managing a worm farm is a great job for kids, giving them plenty of opportunity to indulge their taste for getting dirty. They get their kind of fun; you get the end result for your garden.

You can buy ready-made worm farms from garden centres or hardware shops. They are expensive, but can save time by naturally sorting the castings from the worms. I have had one of these models for the last 10 years – it does a great job of using all kitchen scraps and producing great fertiliser. However, it is easy and more cost effective to make your own worm farm.

To make your own worm farm you only require some basic and easy-to-find equipment. I used some stackable plastic boxes from a home store, a section of garden hose and a seedling tray.

MAKE A WORM FARM: A STEP-BY-STEP GUIDE

Step 1: Materials and tools

You will need:

Materials

- 4 same-size stackable plastic or styrofoam boxes (about 40 cm x 30 cm, or smaller if the worm farm is for only one or two people's scraps); try asking your friendly greengrocer or fish shop for free ones

- 1 5-cm-long piece of garden hose or garden irrigation pipe

- soil, peat or shredded damp newspaper (enough for one box to start)

- 1 small cup of kitchen food scraps (for starters)

- 1 hessian sack, or carpet, or wet newspaper

- 1 cover, e.g. a plastic tray or a piece of wood

- 1000 red or tiger worms (available from commercial worm farmers or even via mail order)

- lime (about a handful per fortnight).

Tools

- cordless drill (or pencil, if using styrofoam boxes).

Step 2: Make a hole in Box 1; insert hose

Take one of the boxes (I'll call this Box 1), and drill or cut a hole towards the bottom of one side. The hole should be just large enough to push the length of garden hose through. Insert the hose – this will drain away the black fluid into a bucket to be used on the garden. Place Box 1 on bricks, rocks or an outdoor table, so that there is room to put a bucket under it. Position it on a slope so the fluid can drain out.

Step 3: Make holes in the remaining boxes

With a cordless drill (a pencil will do if you're using styrofoam boxes), make about 40 small holes in the bottoms of the other three boxes. The holes need to be slightly bigger than a worm. The worms will use these holes to travel up through the stacked boxes. Place one of these boxes (Box 2) on top of Box 1.

Step 4: Add worms and soil

Place soil or peat into Box 2, along with the worms. Sprinkle with water, and spread the kitchen scraps on top of the worms.

Step 5: Cover

Cover Box 2 with the hessian sack, newspaper or carpet, followed by the lid. (I then place a brick on the lid to stop my greedy Labrador helping herself to the food scraps.) A cover is important, as worms like a dark, moist environment. It also stops the birds eating your livestock.

Step 6: Continue feeding until Box 2 is full

Continue to feed the worms until Box 2 is full right to the top. Worms eat their own body weight each day (a bit like me at Christmas!). When Box 2 is full, take off the sack, newspaper or carpet and place Box 3 on top of Box 2. Add a handful of cut-up food scraps. The worms will wriggle their way into their new penthouse to reach new food.

Step 7: Continue until Box 4 is nearly full

When Box 3 is full, repeat Step 6 above with Boxes 3 and 4. When Box 4 is nearly full, Box 2 is ready to use on the garden. Take Box 2 out of the stack and place it on top of Box 4, without a lid, in the sun. This will make any remaining worms move down into Box 4 away from the light.

The completed worm farm. This size worm farm is perfect for a couple or a single person. If you have a large family, use larger boxes such as fish bins.

See how it's done

Watch me demonstrate how to harvest mature vermicasts without harming any of your worms at:
http://www.youtube.com/watch?v=BKJHlhOoF40

TIPS AND TRICKS FOR THE WORM FARMER

- Use the fluid that drains into the bucket on your plants. You can dilute it up to 50 per cent. If you need more fluid straight away, you can pour a bucket of water straight through the farm.

- Worms like a temperature of 15–20°C. It is best to situate the worm bin in a shady position in summer, and in a sunny position in winter. Worms are more active in warm weather, so feed them less in winter.

- In colder climates you can keep the worm farm in the garage.

- Apply a handful of lime to the top bin every fortnight or so to stop the environment from getting too acidic.

- Anything that was once living can be used in the farm, including hair, egg cartons and shells, coffee grounds and paper. Worms don't like citrus or onions.

- The worms will double their population within about 18 months. In two to three years, worm concentrations will reach capacity at about 15,000–20,000 worms.

- These sorts of worms can't survive in normal garden soil, so don't 'set them free'.

- You might find lots of other creepy crawlies living in your worm farm, such as black beetles and tiny flies. They are also beneficial as they help to break down the food.

- If everything is turning smelly and slimy, you are overfeeding.

- A well-run worm farm will have no odour.

- The pH of vermicast (the final product) is neutral. It is great to add to potting mix or as a side dressing for growing plants.

- You can successfully leave the worms for up to three weeks without feeding them. Water them well and make sure they are placed in the shade. Drying out is the biggest threat.

- If ants become a problem, stand each leg of your worm farm in a small bucket of water. The ants won't be able to swim across the moat.

Go on and do your bit for recycling whilst improving the health of your plants and garden soil. Have fun naming all those new pets!

CHICKENS

Chickens are the 'new black' in green urban living. A few hens make a very useful addition to any self-sustaining garden. They will eat all your kitchen leftovers whilst doing your weeding and fertilising, not to mention providing you with daily fresh eggs. And even the smallest townhouse garden can accommodate a couple of bantams, which require only 1.5 square metres of living space each.

13 REASONS TO KEEP CHICKENS

In case you're not yet sold on chickens, here are 13 really good reasons to get some.

1 Willing workers to do all your gardening: If you set up your vegetable garden in a particular way, chickens will do almost all your weeding, fertilising, pest control and mulching, leaving you the fun bits such as seed raising, planting and harvesting, and, of course, eating! Gone are the days when you needed to wheelbarrow expensive compost into your vegetable garden – let the chickens do it for you. I love sitting on my couch, looking through the window and gardening vicariously, watching my chooks in their chicken tractor.

2 Never a dull moment: Each chicken has its own personality. Most are adorable and lovable, the odd one not so! They're also eye-candy, parading their colours, patterns and stripes around the garden.

3 Reconnect with nature: Chickens let us spend time with nature even when we are in the middle of a city. Keeping a few in your backyard allows you to live a greener, more sustainable lifestyle.

4 Have a healthy, chemical-free lawn:
Chickens LOVE to range free, and they'll reduce the amount of lawn mowing you do because they like to eat grass. They'll also eat any lawn pest they can get their beaks on, and they'll turn it all into treasure in the form of little parcels of fertiliser. As long as the chickens are moved regularly they will not scratch up your lawn. Sit in a lounger with a good book and a cold chardonnay while they do the hard work for you. If you use a chicken tractor (see page 142), move the chooks every three or four days when they are on the lawn, rake up their droppings and throw them on the garden.

TOP TIP

Use boiling water and salt to kill lawn weeds.

5 Kitchen leftovers become free food:
Chickens can eat almost anything people can; in fact my chooks much prefer our leftovers to their grain. They are the Labradors of the poultry world! Get a small-lidded bucket for the kitchen and throw those unwanted leftovers into it. No more feeling guilty about letting them rot in the fridge or throwing them out. Watch out for the garlic and onion, though, unless you want your eggs tasting funny. You could also collect food scraps from your neighbours or greengrocer.

TOP TIP

Shared by Woody, Green Community Forum

Put a few drops of colloidal silver in the chickens' drinking water as a general tonic. You can buy this at health-food shops.

6 Tasty, rich, healthy, orange-yolked eggs:
Cats and dogs make great pets, but do they produce anything that is edible? Chickens earn their keep, and once you've dined on their eggs you'll never buy from the supermarket again. They're much tastier, because you can eat them while they are so fresh. Your chickens' yolks will be a rich orange colour because of the varied diet and all the greens they eat. Furthermore, research shows that chickens that are allowed to free range and eat grass lay eggs that are higher in omega-3 fatty acids and vitamin E than most store-bought eggs.

Different breeds of hens lay slightly different-coloured eggs, so if you keep a few different breeds you'll get a basket of rainbow eggs.

TOP TIP

To check if an egg is fresh, shake it. If you can hear sloshing, throw it out. Or place an egg in a bowl of water: if it sinks it is fresh; if it stands up on end it is still OK to eat; if it floats put it straight into the worm farm or compost.

7 Great compost makers: Chicken droppings are nitrogen rich and a great addition to your compost. Eggshells are also great in your compost or worm farm, adding vital calcium to the organic mix.

8 Leaf, weed, and grass clipping on-site disposal:
Stop paying for green waste collection. Leaves, weeds and grass clippings are a treat for chickens. They'll happily dig through whatever you give them, eat what they can, and mulch the rest.

TOP TIP

Shared by Penngt, Green Community Forum

If you want to encourage egg production, feed your chickens Wandering Willy (*Tradescantia*) for eggs the size of an emu's! Keeps the garden tidy too.

9 Save a chicken from an A4-sized cage:
If you're aware of conditions in factory farms, even in some of the 'free-range' farms, I needn't say more. If you're not, please research it. Factory farming is terrifyingly cruel. Each chicken has an allotted A4-sized space in which to spend its short miserable life. If more of us keep chickens there is less demand for those sorts of eggs.

This young chick will grow up a happy chook.
Enjoy your own fresh eggs from your happy chooks.

10 Chickens are the *low*-maintenance pets:

Chickens don't need to be walked, brushed, or fed twice a day. They don't require yearly registrations or costly vet bills. Essentially all you have to do is feed them and gather their eggs daily, and fill their water containers a couple of times a week. How easy is that?

TOP TIP

Shared by bslct, Green Community Forum

My best chicken-keeping tip is to create a 'chicken garden' just outside the pen, then you can pick a few green leaves as you go in to feed them. My chicken garden is in a bath, and it includes medicinal plants that are good for chooks such as tansy, comfrey, kale and spinach. It also contains climbing spinach (basella), which provides shade, and which they can pick at through the fence. It's easy to compost the chicken garden with droppings on the way out, too.

11 Be the greenest kid on the block:

Despite their many merits, backyard chickens are still relatively uncommon. Surprise neighbours, friends and family by being the first person they know to have chickens. Entice them with your lovely home baking, and gift them a few eggs. Soon they will be fellow chicken keepers. Chickens can become great community builders. Neighbours' children love watching your chooks, and I find it is never difficult to find someone to look after our chickens when we go away. The promise of some free fresh eggs is great payment.

12 On-site organic pest disposal units:

Your chickens will eat green vegetable bugs, slugs, snails, flies, centipedes, cockroaches, caterpillars and spiders. In fact all manner of creepy crawlies will be hungrily consumed, avoiding the need for nasty chemicals in your garden.

13 Chickens make great kids' pets:

Chickens are gentle but robust. Importantly, they help teach children about responsibility and nurturing. They are the most eco-green pet to have.

See how it's done

Watch Edwin collect eggs from our chicken tractor at:
www.youtube.com/watch?v=Z4zDEUaWB_I

RULES AND REGULATIONS

Generally speaking, you are allowed to keep between 6 and 12 hens in an urban garden. Roosters aren't allowed, for obvious reasons. (A hen doesn't need a rooster to produce eggs; her eggs will just be infertile.)

Permanent runs need to be 2–3 metres off the boundary, and 10 metres from the dwelling. The coop needs to have a concrete floor. If you choose to keep your chooks in a movable run, you obviously don't need a concrete floor. Officially all poultry have to be contained at all times, but 'gurbers' will admit to letting them free range around the garden at times.

TOP TIP

Write the date you collected your egg on the shell in pencil. This way you will know how old it is.

Most councils are very 'pro' people keeping poultry, and do prefer the movable chicken run system as this avoids a build-up of smells and flies. Most complaints from neighbours are as a result of people not cleaning out coops regularly, with smells and flies therefore becoming a problem. If you decide to keep your chooks in a permanent run, ensure you design a coop that is easy to get into to clean.

To check your council's regulations, go to their website and search under *by-laws: poultry*.

TOP TIP

Make an outside flytrap

Cut off the lower three-quarters of a plastic drink bottle. Put in some pieces of meat and half fill with warm water. Invert the neck of the bottle (the remaining quarter) into the lower section, creating a funnel – the flies will crawl down it and become trapped. Place in a sunny spot. The flies will drown or die from the heat. Empty and repeat.

Chickens don't require a lot of space if you house them in a movable run. A good rule of thumb is one square metre for every chicken in a run, or three square metres per chicken in a permanent coop. You only need half that for bantams.

Chickens need to be part of a flock, so you must keep at least two or three birds to be kind. Three is best, then if you lose one, the survivor is not left on her own. Three to four layers will keep a family well supplied with eggs; keep six to eight hens if you are a baker!

Bantams are around half the size of normal chickens. They are less destructive in the garden, as they do not dig and scratch as much. Bantams do lay eggs, but not in great numbers – and the eggs are smaller.

Chickens sleep by perching off the ground. Provide at least 25 cm of perching space per bird. Chickens will try to get to the top perch – top perch means you are top dog (so to speak). To prevent nightly squabbling for the highest perch, have all your perches at the same level.

Bantams are around half the size of normal chickens. They are less destructive in the garden, as they do not dig and scratch as much. Bantams do lay eggs, but not in great numbers – and the eggs are smaller.

TOP CHICKEN BREEDS FOR URBAN GARDENS

Many people new to chickens think they only come in brown. This is probably because of the widespread use of the battery hen breed, known as Brown Shavers, Red Shavers or Hyline Brown, millions of which are kept for egg production. These battery-type breeds are easier to come by than heritage breeds – these were the first chickens I ever kept for that very reason. They are noisy, particularly when they have just laid an egg, and never go broody – which may be good or bad.

Luckily there are other, heritage, breeds to choose from. These are the breeds I recommend if you live in town. They are relatively quiet and docile, and make great gardeners. They produce good amounts of tasty fresh eggs and do occasionally go broody, happily hatching any fertile eggs, enabling you to increase your stock. They are long-lived, so are good to keep as pets.

Consider some of the following older breeds: Light Sussex; Orpington; Barnevelder; Wyandotte; Barred Plymouth Rock; Dorking. Many are now quite rare, so in keeping these we are not only helping to keep the breeds established, but keeping a little history alive in our garden.

HOW LONG DO CHICKENS LIVE FOR?

A purebred hen can live to be well over eight years old. The older they get the fewer eggs they lay, but think of all the mulching, fertilising, pest control and weed eating they provide. Battery farm breeds are not so long-lived. After about three years of age many suffer prolapses or become egg bound (the eggs get stuck inside the chicken). Their bodies are often exhausted by the huge number of eggs they have laid during their short life.

WHERE TO BUY CHICKENS

You can buy 'point of lay' chickens (teenagers about to start laying) from many battery chicken farms or online auction sites, or ask around to find local breeders. The price of purebred chickens ranges from about $20 to over $50. Hyline Browns are normally around $18. Remember, Hyline Browns will lay well for two years and then they are basically 'spent'; purebreds will keep laying well into old age, which is about eight years old.

- To find chickens in online auction sites look under farming and then poultry.

- The magazine *Lifestyle Block* sometimes advertises breeders.

- If you see a poultry show advertised in your region, go along for a visit. It's a great way to check out all the amazing breeds, and there are always chickens for sale at very good prices.

- www.rarebreeds.co.nz is a website worth visiting to find breeders of purebred chickens.

If you would like to give a home to an ex battery chicken, visit www.chickenrescue.net.nz

Housing your chickens

Chickens are happy in cold and frosty weather, but they do require a shelter to escape cold winds and rain. They require perches to sleep on at night, and a small box to lay eggs in. They need protection from predators, which in town are mainly dogs. Don't worry about the neighbourhood cats – a fully grown chicken can look after itself with any domestic feline.

A mobile pen allows you to put your chickens to work in the vegetable garden or to keep the grass short on your lawn. A mobile pen also prevents the build-up of smells, flies and chicken manure, and does away with the weekly chore of mucking out of coops.

The more traditional permanent enclosed chicken coop and attached run can be put to good use by creating a 'deep litter' system for the chooks to work through (see page 111?). If you want to keep your chooks using this system, design a chicken coop that is easy to clean out.

When I first got our chickens, the neighbourhood cats would circle around their run like hunting sharks. The minute I let my chooks out to free range all the cats took off in fright! Our cat is now best friends with the hens, and I often have to remove him from the laying box, where he likes to sleep during the day, so the hens can lay their eggs.

A traditional permanent coop and run in a suburban backyard.

See how it's done

Watch Dave, a fellow 'gurber', explain his design of a permanent chicken coop in his urban backyard at:

www.youtube.com/watch?v=ABTAGi9hPqc

and watch him demonstrate how he cleans out his chicken coop at:

www.youtube.com/watch?v=IKPJ_6EEZSg

Bedding

A thick layer of bedding material in each laying box will provide a comfortable place for your hens to lay their eggs. The soft bedding material also helps prevent eggs from rolling and breaking. There are many materials to choose from, including pine wood shavings, straw and pine needles. Pine needles, lavender, tansy, rue, fennel, wormwood and rosemary stalks will all deter mites and lice.

TOP TIP

Shared by Kayo, Green Community Forum

Collect the lint from the clothes dryer and use it to line the chooks' nesting boxes. It is soft, and the chooks love nestling into it to lay their daily eggs. A great use for a waste product.

If you have battery farm hens, you may find they try to sleep in their laying box rather than on the perches. This is because they have so far spent their life on the floor, and never had a mother to teach them how to behave like a proper chicken. You don't want chickens sleeping in the laying boxes, as their droppings will soil the eggs. To cure this habit you need to go out just after dusk each night, physically remove the chickens from the boxes and place them on the perches. You may need to repeat this for more than a week. You can also try putting something (e.g. a box or a stuffed plastic bag) inside the laying box each night to prevent the chooks from getting into the space. Just remember to remove it early each morning so they can lay their morning eggs.

You may find that all your hens will use the same laying box to lay their eggs in. I keep eight chooks in my large 'chicken tractor' and have only one laying box, which they happily share. They take turns to lay in the box each morning. It can be a little like watching a large family waiting for the one available bathroom, with some chooks hopping from one foot to the other, waiting patiently. Occasionally things get really desperate and I find two hens in the box trying to lay at the same time!

TOP TIP

Remove the innards from that old unused computer or box-shaped TV and use as a laying box for chooks. This gives it another life and prevents it from going to landfill. Lawnmower catchers also make great laying boxes.

What about rats?

Many people believe chickens and rats go hand in hand. This doesn't have to be the case: here are some ways to prevent nasty vermin from coming onto your property.

- Feed chooks any food scraps in the morning, so it is eaten by nightfall.

- Don't feed chooks any meat or dairy products.

- Remove any uneaten food scraps from the run before nightfall; put them in the worm farm.

- Keep the area clean.

- Keep the poultry grain in a tightly sealed, ratproof container.

TOP TIP

Rats and mice hate the smell of tar, so soak some rags in tar and scatter around the compost heap.

Dust baths

Chickens love to take dust baths. On a sunny day they will dig a shallow hole, loosen up all the dirt, and proceed to get themselves as dirty and dusty as they possibly can. This is a hen's version of a day spa! Dust baths are absolutely necessary – they prevent parasites such as mites and lice.

Chickens love dust baths and will choose a favourite spot in your garden to take their daily bath.

If your chickens don't free range, or their run area doesn't have a dry patch of ground where they can dig a hole, you'll need to provide them with an artificial dust bath. Place a shallow box on the floor of their coop and fill it with 20 cm of a homemade dusting powder. This recipe will help kill any lice organically as the chickens have their baths. It is especially handy if your chooks are hard to catch when you need to de-louse them.

Ingredients:

- 2 parts fireplace ashes (untreated wood)

- 2 parts sand

- 1 part diatomaceous earth (see page 43)

TOP TIP

Your eggs may have traces of dirt or chicken faeces on them. Resist the urge to scrub them clean – eggs are very porous and you risk forcing any bacteria into the egg. If you're one of those people who need perfect-looking eggs, rub them very gently with your fingers under warm water just before using. Wash your hands thoroughly.

To produce a reasonable number of tasty eggs, chickens require good-quality food. If you feed them only kitchen scraps, you won't get many eggs.

A hen will eat around 1.5 cups of grain each day, less if they are fed weeds and kitchen leftovers. It's easiest to purchase 'complete' feeds that have exactly the right mix of vitamins, minerals, proteins, carbohydrates and fat. Feeds come in both organic and conventional varieties. If your chickens have started laying eggs or are 20 weeks or older, purchase a complete 'layer' feed. If they're younger than that, you'll need a complete 'starter' feed.

Dinner time!

TOP TIP

Shared by Woody, Green Community Forum

I give my chooks jelly meat and cottage cheese as a treat. They love it, and it's full of protein. When the weather's damp I collect snails in a bucket, and in the morning feed them to the chooks.

Poultry need constant access to fresh, clean water. If they are denied water for any length of time, they quickly become stressed and stop laying. I use a two-litre plastic milk bottle laid on its side with a hole cut in the top. I find the chickens can't kick it over and can't flick dirt into it with all their scratching.

Chickens prefer cold water, so place the container in a shady area of their run.

TOP TIP

Put some limestone pebbles or finely crushed eggshells in the chickens' drinking water. This helps provide daily calcium and, along with grit, will keep eggshells strong.

I give my chooks kitchen scraps in the morning and pellets in the afternoon, so they go to bed with a full crop (the pouch where food is stored before digestion) ready to lay an egg in the morning. I feed the chickens with pellets rather than mash – the pellets stay in the chickens' crops longer so they feel satisfied longer. I find that if I feed the chickens whole grains, like wheat or oats, when they are on the vegetable beds, I get wheat and oat grass sprouting everywhere.

Buy pellets for layers from farm-supply stores. You may need to travel to the fringe of large cities to find these shops. Some supermarkets stock chicken food in the pet food aisle; some pet shops also stock chicken pellets. Buying a 35 kg bulk sack is the cheapest option.

It is really difficult to find organic poultry pellets, but if you do want to go totally organic it is sometimes easier to buy organic wheat. Sprouted wheat is more nutritious, so you could set up a system for sprouting, as follows:

- Lay a hessian sack on the ground and wet with water.

- Sprinkle the wheat thickly over the sacking and then cover with another sack.

- Keep moist until it germinates.

- Place the sack, complete with germinating wheat, in the coop for your poultry to eat. They will peck and scratch at the sacking, eating all the grain.

- Remove the sacking and repeat.

Another method is to use lidded buckets: half-fill a bucket with wheat and enough water to dampen. The wheat will sprout in three to four days. Feed to chooks when sprouting. Have the next sprouted wheat bucket ready to go when that one is finished. If you are sprouting wheat in a bucket, make sure you change the water at least twice a day or it will start to ferment and you will end up distilling a brew of 'moonshine' rather than chook food!

Where to find grain

Organic poultry grain suppliers:
www.biograins.co.nz

Foods chickens shouldn't eat

Don't feed these to your chickens:

- citrus fruits and peelings
- bones – they will attract rodents
- any large serving of meat, or meat that has gone bad
- garlic and onion (unless you want your eggs tasting of them)
- morning glories and daffodils – these are poisonous to chickens, and even though chickens will generally know to avoid them, you might just want to keep an eye on them around these plants.

Grit

Chickens don't have teeth! Instead they store grit – small rocks or shells – in their crop, where it helps to break up food ready for digestion. Grit also replaces calcium that hens lose daily when producing eggs. Keep a small container of oyster grit accessible to your chickens, or mix a small amount in with their daily grain.

To stop the chooks kicking over the grit container, I use a hopper made out of an old child's gumboot. Cut the toe out of the gumboot, fill the boot with grit and then suspend it in the run. The hens can peck at it as needed, but won't waste the grit.

You can buy grit at the same place you buy grain. Or collect sand and small pieces of shell from the beach. If you eat oysters or mussels, save the shells, dry them in the sun and smash into small pieces with a hammer.

PESTS AND DISEASES

As long as your chickens are kept in clean living quarters and dry conditions, they should remain healthy. However, if a chicken shows any of the following symptoms, there may be a problem:

- mangy appearance
- quiet and huddled, away from the flock
- visible mites
- abnormal droppings, including blood, visible worms, diarrhoea, droppings that are all white (normal stool is brown with a white cap)
- sneezing
- loss of energy
- sudden, drastic reduction of position in pecking order
- loss of appetite
- stunted growth.

Lice

A really bad infestation of lice can cause anaemia due to loss of blood, and a decrease in egg production. To check a hen for lice, turn the bird gently upside down and pull back the feathers around her bottom. Lice look like moving little brown grains of rice. You can buy bird lice powder from the pet shop. You could also try derris dust (from the garden centre) or diatomaceous earth. Dust powder around their bottom and under each wing.

Mites

Mites look like tiny spiders. They live in the cracks of wooden perches during the day and move onto the chickens' legs at night to feast. Clean the perches every six months with a pyrethrum solution: mix 10 ml of pyrethrum spray (from the garden centre) with a litre of water and a squirt of washing-up liquid. Thoroughly spray all internal walls and perches of the coop. Pay particular attention to corners, cracks and any splits in the wood – this is where the little vampires live. I also sprinkle Flowers of Sulphur powder (also from the garden centre) around and on the perches.

Scaly leg mite

This condition is caused by mites living under the scales of the chickens' legs. Infected hens have raised scales on their legs. Scrub affected legs with a pyrethrum solution to kill the mites – an old toothbrush is perfect for this. Make up a solution of 5 ml of pyrethrum in a litre of warm water. After scrubbing both legs you can cover the legs with Vaseline, which will help to contain the solution and suffocate the mites.

TOP TIP

Shared by Woody, Green Community Forum

Rub scabies cream on any chooks with scaly leg mites, and then cover with Vaseline.

Worms

Free-ranging birds enjoy many benefits and privileges over those kept in coops and cages. However, these lucky chickens can suffer from a few extra illnesses, the main one being intestinal worms. You can buy worming treatments from the vet, but most are derived from nasty chemicals rendering the eggs inedible for up to seven days. This is my organic solution to worming chooks: crush four large garlic cloves and add to the chickens' drinking water with a splash of cider vinegar. Make this the only water available to the chickens for three days, then discard and replace with fresh water. Do this every two months. Garlic changes the conditions in a hen's gut, making it less hospitable for intestinal worms.

You can also feed finely chopped garlic tops to your poultry. The birds will generally eat only what they need. Remember, however, that garlic is rich in sulphur, therefore excessive garlic shouldn't be given to hens that are laying or the smell will taint the eggs.

The following mash is another worming recipe – this quantity is enough for one chook, so increase for the number in your flock.

Anti-worm mash

- 1 handful of wormwood (*Artemisia sp.*)

- 1 handful of tansy plant (*Tanacetum vulgarum*) tips

- 1 comfrey leaf

- 1 cup grated carrot

- 1 cup crushed layers' pellets

- 5 cloves garlic

- water

Finely chop the wormwood, comfrey leaf and tansy tips. Add the chopped leaves, grated carrot and crushed garlic to a cup of pellets. Mix with a little warm water to make a mash, and feed the mixture as the only food for two days. Repeat every second month.

Remember to worm all your chooks at the same time. Make sure to worm any new arrivals, as they could have worms that will spread to your worm-free chickens.

Nasturtium seeds are also a good wormer (plus they have a tonic, antiseptic and medicinal action). The chickens will eat only what they need, so you can experiment to determine how much that is – observe amounts left over and adjust rations accordingly. The seeds can be preserved in vinegar.

Pumpkin seeds contain a chemical that paralyses worms, which are then expelled from the chicken's gut. (They are a good natural wormer for humans, too.)

Nasturtium flowers develop into caper-like seeds at the end of summer. Feed these to your chooks as a wormer.

GENERAL CHICKEN CARE

Introducing new birds to the flock

Adding new stock to an established flock can be stressful. Your established flock all know their pecking order. When newbies arrive every hen will once again have to fight for her spot on the pecking ladder. All-out war may break out, but normally only lasts for five to seven days.

If you have a run, put the new birds in with your old-timers, but separate them with chicken wire or shade cloth. This lets them eyeball each other without having physical contact. Do this for a week before introducing them to the flock.

Here are some other ideas to distract them – rather like you would a two-year-old child!

- Introduce new hens at night.

- Introduce at least two new hens at a time – safety in numbers.

- Hang a head of cauliflower or cabbage just out of reach so the chickens have to jump to get at it. This helps keep their mind on other things.

- Add large branches, or rolls of chicken wire, to the run (and inside the coop if possible): this makes pursuit more difficult and gives the new hens a place to hide.

- Add dead leaves, grass clippings, pulled weeds and/ or table scraps to their run to give them plenty to dig through, helping them forget about the new hens.

An even better distraction is to let them free range. Your flock will be far too interested in the prospect of worms, insects and weeds to bother about each other. They won't go back in the coop until dusk, at which point they'll be settling in for a night's sleep and won't be so motivated to harass one another. (Don't do this until the newcomers have spent at least seven days on your property so they know it's 'home', otherwise you may have a runaway bird on your hands.)

Winter egg production

Due to fewer daylight hours in winter, your chickens' egg production will decrease. If you want more eggs, provide your girls with supplemental light during the otherwise dark morning and early evening hours – chooks need 12 hours of daylight per day to keep laying. I use a solar-powered light and turn it on in the late afternoon. It runs for about four hours before it goes flat, to be recharged the following day. Aim to provide a light the strength of a 60 watt bulb.

Broodiness

Your hens may go 'broody' at any time in their life. This is when they stubbornly insist on sitting on eggs in order to hatch them into baby chicks. It doesn't matter if the eggs are fertilised or not; some hens will even go broody on golf balls or large stones! (The Hyline Brown (Brown Shaver), however, rarely goes broody – that trait has been bred out.)

Our Light Sussex 'Happy Feet' went broody. I bought some fertile eggs, which arrived in the post, each perfectly bubble wrapped with no breakages. After 21 days our new chicks began to hatch. New-born chicks are a wonderful experience for children – I never get tired of the sight, either.

A broody hen is a pain for a number of reasons. She will sit and sit, and be grumpy if you try and disturb her. She won't eat or lay eggs. If she is allowed to sit on fresh eggs, the heat of her body can quickly rot them. Also, she will not allow the other hens to use the laying box.

To prevent this habit from forming, collect eggs every day – hens are more likely to go broody on a nest full of eggs.

If a hen becomes broody, there are several tricks you can use. Start by repeatedly removing her from the nest. When Bluey, our Orpington, goes broody, we remove her and carry her around for ten minutes or so, five times a day. We have to do this for two days before she stops. For birds that are more determined to be mums, ice cubes or an ice pack in the nest will usually do the trick. In rare cases, more extreme measures are necessary. Putting the hen in a wire cage and hanging her in a tree in the shade can work – the air under her lower parts cures her.

Moulting

Once a year chickens shed and regrow some of their feathers. This process is called 'moulting', and it usually happens in autumn. During this time they look like a flea-bitten feather duster and they definitely won't lay eggs. Don't worry – this isn't a sign of illness! The feathers will grow back thick and glossy. Nettles, comfrey and sunflower seeds all provide natural minerals to help grow beautiful glossy plumage. Remember you will need to clip your chooks' wings after their moult.

Interestingly a sign of a good layer is the hen that moults the fastest. Those of your flock that take forever to finally get rid of the old feathers and grow new ones are probably not the best layers. During this time the hen is putting all her energy into growing new feathers so will stop laying for about six weeks.

Clipping wings

Wings are clipped to prevent chickens flying over fences or boundaries. To do this spread out one wing, and, with a pair of sharp scissors, cut along the stiff, long flight feathers at the tip of the wing about five centimetres from where they come out of the skin. This does not hurt the chicken. Only clip one wing, as this will unbalance the chook when she tries to fly. You need to do this once a year after each moult.

Using a sharp pair of scissors, clip the long flight feathers of one wing. This does not hurt the chicken.

See how it's done

Watch me demonstrate how to safely clip your chickens' wings at:
www.youtube.com/watch?v=BPyorFmbYIM

A FEW THINGS *NOT* TO WORRY ABOUT

- Your chickens' first eggs: these will be pretty pathetic! They'll be small, the shells will be weak and some won't have shells at all. Don't worry – this is not a sign of sickness.

- A double-yolk egg: think yourself lucky.

- Moulting (see above).

- A tiny speck of blood in an egg – this is normal.

A chicken tractor with a brustix roof. The perches are located under the roof area.

MAKE A CHICKEN TRACTOR: A STEP-BY-STEP GUIDE

WHY HAVE A CHICKEN TRACTOR?

No weeding, no digging, no spraying, no worries: want to know more? Let chickens do these jobs by making them a 'chicken tractor' – a great solution for time-poor urban gardeners.

A chicken tractor is a mobile chicken run about the same size as your vegetable garden beds. The chickens are put onto the garden beds inside their chicken tractor after you have harvested your vegetables. One chicken tractor can easily provide total maintenance for 10–15 vegetable beds. After the initial time and cost spent building the tractor, all you need to do is spend ten minutes moving the tractor every three weeks or so. The result is rich, fertile, black, sweet-smelling soil that grows anything and is teeming with worms.

The chickens can live in the tractor year round. This rotational system generally sees them on each garden bed three to four times a year, and when the chicken tractor isn't on the vegetable beds, you can move them around the lawn.

The chicken tractor can house baby chicks or mature hens, keeping them safe from urban predators such as dogs.

The instructions that follow are for a rectangular-shaped chicken run measuring 2.75 m x 1.25 m. This can comfortably house three large hens. You can modify the dimensions to suit your own vegetable bed shape and number of chickens, but you should allow around one square metre of space per chicken. You can find all the equipment at the hardware store, but get your recycling thinking cap on and see what materials you have lying around that could be used.

Step 1: Materials and equipment

You don't require any fancy building tools or skills, and can make this tractor in an afternoon. It is made out of PVC piping, which can be found at recycling yards or plumbing shops. Being light, one person can easily move the tractor around the lawn, and two people can easily lift it onto a raised bed.

- 8 m of 32 mm-wide PVC piping (this normally comes in 6 m lengths
- 4 x 32 mm PVC joining elbows
- 16 m of 20 mm PVC piping
- 4 x 20 mm PVC elbows
- about 100 cable ties
- 12 m (approx) roll of chicken wire (see Top Tip below)
- light, waterproof covering for the roof (e.g. a tarpaulin or real estate signs)
- branches or wooden poles (for perches)
- small piece of bungy cord (to fasten door)
- 3 m of galvanised wire (12 gauge or similar)
- 1 plastic box or lawn mower catcher (to use as laying box)
- PVC glue
- 3 m of UV-resistant twine (baling twine is good)

Tools:

- handsaw
- drill (hand or battery powered)
- wire cutters
- scissors

TOP TIP

Buy the small-gauge chicken wire (the one with the smallest holes) so that wild birds can't get through and eat the chicken food. I also prefer plastic-coated chicken wire, as it's gentler on the hands.

Step 2: Make the rectangular base frame

With a hand saw, cut the 32 mm PVC piping into two 2.75 m lengths and two 1.25 m lengths. Using the PVC glue, and following directions on the bottle, paint glue into the 32 mm elbow joiners and on the ends of the piping, and glue segments together so that you have a rectangle shape.

Step 3: Form arches along the run

Cut the 20 mm PVC into four 2.5 m lengths (these will form the arches over the rectangular base frame). Fix arches to either end of the base frame as follows: form an arch by curving a length, and place the ends inside the base frame. Drill a small horizontal hole through the base frame and both ends of one arch, and fix with galvanised wire. Repeat this at the other end. Measure one metre in from both ends, mark, and fix arches at these positions in the same way. You need about eight pairs of hands to help hold up these arches, so find some friends! You will finish with four arches along the base frame.

Step 4: Add the top rail

Cut another piece of 20 mm PVC piping measuring 2.9 m long. Weave this length under and over the four arches. (The extra length at each end creates handles for lifting or sliding the run.) Drill a hole and use galvanised wire to hold each arch in place.

Step 5: Apply bracing

Apply the UV-resistant twine to the inside of the two middle arches, level with the ground. This gives the structure some strength and keeps it square. Cut the twine to length and tie it onto the base rail with a strong knot.

The elbow joiners that help form the rectangular shape on the base frame.

The top rail is weaved through the arches. The bracing is on the two middle arches – this is the black rope that stretches across the ground. The roof covers the end third of the enclosure.

Bracing is secured to the bases of the two middle arches. Note how the arches are secured to the inside of the base frame.

Step 6: Make the door rail

Decide where you want the door. A good position is in the middle of one side at ground level. That way you can leave the door open for the chickens to free range. Measure and cut a 750 mm length of 20 mm PVC piping and position it horizontally between the two middle arches, 300 mm up from the base rail. Drill holes and fix with galvanised wire. (If you have adjusted the measurements of the run, double-check the length of door required to fit between the two middle arches.) This rail provides bracing and something to attach the chicken wire to. The 750 mm x 300 mm space will form the space for the hinged door.

Step 7: Put on the chicken wire

Fix chicken wire over the structure, except for the door space. If dogs aren't a problem, use cable ties to fix the chicken wire to the structure, or to make it more secure, weave galvanised wire through the chicken wire and framing. If roaming dogs are an issue in your neighbourhood, you can make the run extra secure by extending the chicken wire down past the base frame and creating a 'skirt' of chicken wire around the run. Lie this flat on the ground and secure with tent pegs to prevent any dogs digging under the run.

Step 8: Install perches

Cut branches or poles to the width of the run (I use bamboo or branches cut from trees). The recommended perch diameter is 50 mm (this can be smaller for bantams); allow 250 mm of roosting space per chicken. Drill holes and wire them onto the framing at one end, at least 500 mm off the ground. Ensure the chooks have at least 400mm of headroom when they are on the perches. Secure the perch at both ends; chickens prefer a solid perch rather than swinging like a budgie!

Step 9: Put in a laying box

Place a box in the run for the chickens to lay their eggs in. A lawn mower catcher works well, or you can use a plastic box on its side, secured to the end of the run by some extra 20 mm piping framing. If you cut a hole in the back of the box you can collect the eggs without having to reach into the run. Fasten the door with a small piece of bungy cord.

Step 10: Add a waterproof roof

The simplest way to cover the perching area is with a tarpaulin. Secure with bungy cords or sew onto the framing. Another option is to use real estate signs: ask any real estate agent – they normally have plenty lying around as they are not reusable. Cut them to width, drill holes, bend them over the framing and secure with cable ties. Make sure that whatever covering you use reaches lower than the perches to give the chooks protection from the wind and rain; extend the roof structure down to the ground at the back if you live in a cold area. Cut semicircle shapes for the front and back sections.

Step 11: Make a door

Cut 20 mm PVC into four lengths to form a frame measuring 750 mm x 300 mm. Fix together using the four elbow joiners and glue. Cover with chicken wire using cable ties. Drill two holes into the bottom of the frame, and use some wire to hinge it to the base rail. Secure the door with a bungy tie.

A laying box that you can access from outside makes daily egg collection easy. A piece of bungy cord keeps the flap shut. I have covered the perching area with brustix just for looks; you could use coffee sacks or painted real estate signs.

Added extras

To make moving the run a breeze, you could add two small wheels to one end, then it's just a matter of lifting the other end and dragging the run along the ground.

Adapting for other micro-livestock

This run can also be modified to house rabbits and guinea pigs – just extend the chicken wire under the run. It could also be used to house quail or ducks.

And finally ...

While your vegetables are still growing, don't weed or pull out anything that has gone to seed, as this provides food for the chickens while they are cleaning up the area. If there are any bare areas in the garden, try sowing some quick-growing mustard seeds as a green manure crop and chicken food.

While your chicken tractor is on a vegetable bed, add all your kitchen scraps, grass clippings, coffee grounds, dust from vacuum cleaner bags, ash from the fire, hedge trimmings, weeds and any other organic material. The chickens will eat what they like and scratch and mulch everything else, while adding rich manure to it all. Throw an armful of straw into the mix every week to really get the chooks scratching (this will also help get rid of any composting smells). They will devour any slugs and other insects, and eat any weeds and seeds. After three weeks or so the space should be transformed into beautiful rich organic material ready to plant the next crop straight into.

When the chickens have been moved on, sprinkle some garden lime over the garden and irrigate with a sprinkler for about an hour, giving the area a really good soaking. This encourages all the earthworms to come up into the upper mulch level. When you're ready to plant seedlings, just make a small hole in the mulch and plant directly.

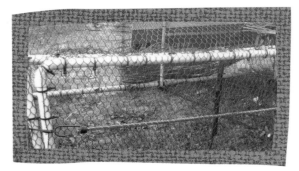

Door closed and secured with a bungy cord. Notice the spacings of the cable ties to firmly secure the netting to the frame. Hinge it at the bottom so you can leave the door open when your chooks are free ranging.

See how it's done

For a quick tiki tour of my chicken tractor, visit: www.youtube.com/watch?v=b8EYD8ThJSl

BEEKEEPING

Bees play a vital role in New Zealand's agriculture and horticulture industries, as well as in our home gardens. Roughly one-third of what we eat is pollinated by bees. There are all sorts of food we wouldn't be able to grow without them, including apples, pears, stone fruit, cucumbers, kiwifruit, berry fruit, and even clover. Alarmingly, bee numbers are declining worldwide.

I love beekeeping. I started two years ago in a bid to help increase the pollination levels of my fruit and vegetables. They are fascinating to watch and a joy to have in the garden. The smallest

townhouse – or even an apartment – can have a hive, as it is the surrounding 'airspace' the bees use. Bees actually fare better in urban areas, as they have year-round and varied nectar and pollen sources to visit. When you consider all the parks, schools, playgrounds, private gardens, planted roundabouts and reserves we have in town, you'll appreciate that bees are treated to an almost year-round banquet of nectar.

Not only are bees important for pollination, they are also highly productive. One hive can harvest around 30 kg of honey each year. Consuming your own local honey is also a good way of combating allergies, especially hay fever. When you eat local honey you consume a small amount of local pollen, which helps to protect you against these allergens. Local honey is also normally raw honey, which means it has not been heat treated, or blended with inferior honey. The result is a natural honey full of all the important vitamins that are often destroyed or diluted during the heating process.

My top-bar hive.

TOP-BAR BEEHIVES

I keep my bees in a top-bar hive. This type of hive has been around for hundreds of years, but has recently become very popular with backyard beekeepers in the USA and the UK. It consists of a long horizontal box with sloping sides, with wooden bars positioned along the top. The bees make their comb on these top bars, and fill it with their young, or honey that you can harvest as beautiful honeycomb.

Top-bar hives are still a new concept in New Zealand – there are many beekeepers here that haven't even heard of them. I like these hives because they are cheap to build, low tech to manage, and provide honeybees with a very natural way to live. There is also no heavy lifting involved, and no extra equipment to store. There is no need to prepare foundation wax or frames, or find a honey extractor to get your honey out of the frames. All you need is the top-bar hive, protective clothing, and a bread knife to help prise off the bars. I don't even use a smoker, as the bees are not as disturbed in the way that they are when you enter a conventional hive, and thus do not become as aggressive.

You don't get as much honey as you do from a Langstroth hive (the standard beehive), but you do get enough to share with friends and family – during summer I harvest around four jars every three weeks. I just crush the honeycomb in a basin with a potato masher and put it through the kitchen sieve to get runny honey. I told you it was low tech!

Your hive will also give you lots of wax for making into furniture polish, creams and candles.

TOP TIP

To make homemade furniture polish, melt half a cup of beeswax with one cup of olive oil and stir for three minutes. Remove from the heat and add lavender oil (or any other essential oil). Transfer into a clean jar and allow the solution to set.

See how it's done

Watch me demonstrate how to handle comb in a top-bar hive at:
www.youtube.com/watch?v=PFmvVRjzKZU

WHERE TO SITE YOUR HIVE

Bees leave the hive on warm sunny mornings to forage. They fly about a metre from the entrance, and then climb steeply into the sky before flying away in all directions. They don't leave en masse as a black cloud, so neighbours are often unaware that you have a hive in your garden.

In urban areas it's important to position your hive so the bees don't create a nuisance to neighbours or passing pedestrians. A high location, such as a shed roof or an apartment balcony, is ideal as it forces the bees to use a high flight path. Another good position is about three metres behind a tall hedge or fence, as this forces the bees to fly high when they exit the hive.

It's important to get the position right first time, as it's difficult to move a hive once the bees are in it. Beekeepers have a saying that you can move a hive half a metre or five kilometres.

The bees build comb down from the top bar and then fill each space up with either nectar, or brood that develop into mature worker bees. Each bee has a particular job to do in the hive; this could be guard, housekeeper or nurse.

The top bars in the hive are full of capped honey (the combs are full of honey and sealed with wax) during summer.

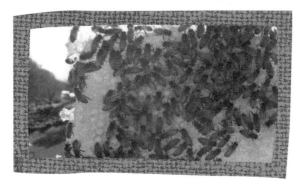

A comb of capped honey ready to harvest. Fresh honeycomb is perfect on toast. It has many health benefits, and, as it is raw and unheated, it retains all its important vitamins.

Bees find their hive through landmarks, so if their hive is moved a couple of metres from its established spot the bees will come back to the original spot and cluster on the ground wondering what fool moved their home.

How to move a beehive

To successfully move a hive you need to wait until dark, when all the workers have returned. Close up the entrance and then move the hive right out of their familiar territory (the area within a five-kilometre radius of the hive). Once the hive is located in a new spot (at least five kilometres away), the bees will leave the hive in the morning and imprint this new site as their new home. After a month or so you can then move the hive back to your garden in its new position.

Which bee?

Life is easier if you keep a docile strain of bee. If your bees are aggressive and fly at your face when you open the hive, you should 'requeen'. The queen passes her genes to all her offspring, so by choosing a more docile strain of queen you change the whole nature of the colony. There are queen bee breeders who specialise in docile queens.

HOW MUCH OF YOUR TIME DO BEES REQUIRE?

Some books state that bees require less time than a pet dog, but more time than a cat. In my experience this is untrue – keeping bees takes hardly any time at all.

Having said that, you can't just put a beehive in your garden and leave the bees to it; they require regular checks and maintenance. Top-bar beehives need to be visited more regularly than a conventional hive. In late spring through summer I visit my hives at least every three weeks to take any capped honey and to check that the bees have enough space for their brood and honey stores. Autumn is a time to treat for varroa (see page 151) and ensure that your bees have enough honey stores to get them through the winter. Winter is the quiet time. The colony numbers decrease, and in colder areas the bees form a huddle to keep warm. The queen stops laying and the drones (males) are booted out the door and not allowed to return. The warmer spring days see the colony go into full population expansion in readiness for when summer plants start tempting them with nectar. This is also the time to again check and treat for any diseases, prevent swarming and make sure your queen has survived the winter.

As you get more confident handling your bees, a visit to the hive to monitor and maybe harvest some honey will take only 20 minutes at the most. Most of that is taken struggling into your bee suit!

Suppliers of beekeeping equipment

www.ecroyd.com

www.bees.co.nz

What about stings?

Stings do happen, but if you're careful they'll be rare. I have been stung only once in two years. I don't care what anyone says – bee stings really HURT! So always wear a bee suit and gloves when attending your hive. Incidentally, bee suits are always white or a light colour as this has a calming effect on the bees. Blue appears to make them more aggressive. Also avoid wearing woollen jerseys around bees – if bees get stuck in the wool they will try and sting. (Perhaps they think you are a bear trying to steal their honey.)

I should also mention that my eldest son is allergic to bee stings – so much so that he requires adrenaline. You may be thinking how irresponsible I am! But having a beehive in our garden has taught him how important they are, that they don't sting without good reason, and that he needs to wear shoes in summer when on the lawn. And he loves visiting the hive and looking through the observation window to see what the bees are doing.

The best time to open the hive is mid-morning on warm still days. 'Warm' here means T-shirt weather – warm enough for the bees to be foraging and for you to expose the brood (baby bees) to the air. (The temperature of a hive is around 35°C, which keeps the brood warm.) Approach a hive from the side or back, never the front, as the bees guarding the entrance will fly at you to protect the colony. Work slowly and gently.

WHERE TO GET YOUR BEES

The easiest thing about beekeeping is getting a hive and protective clothing. The hard part is finding some bees and persuading them to stay in your hive. It is difficult to train 30,000-odd insects.

TOP TIP

If you get stung, gently scrape out the sting with your fingernail, being careful not to squeeze the end of the sting. Apply a compress of vinegar to the site for half an hour.

Apis is a homeopathic remedy that I have taken in the past with good effect. Buy from any homeopathic supplier.

The observation window at the back of the hive is a great feature. You can quickly check on the bees and show visitors what the bees are up to. Kids love looking at the bees.

TOP TIP

Make a natural insect repellent by heating five tablespoons of almond oil and one tablespoon of beeswax in a saucepan. When melted, take off heat and add one teaspoon each of eucalyptus oil, and lavender and lemon-grass essential oils. Store in a small glass jar. Wipe on pulse points and around ankles.

Catch a swarm

The cheapest way to start beekeeping is to catch a swarm. This may sound a bit daunting, but usually it is a relatively simple process. When a new queen hatches, the old queen and half the workforce leave the hive to find a new place to take up residence. This is called *swarming*. It is the bees' natural way to increase their numbers.

The old queen will land on a tree branch or other object while scout bees search for new quarters.

All the workers form a tight cluster around the queen. This normally looks like a rugby ball. It is a simple process to hold a box or similar container under the swarm, while wearing your bee suit, and to gently knock or shake the cluster of bees into the box. As long as the queen drops into the box, the swarm will normally stay. Cover the top of the box with empty top bars from the hive, leaving a small entry hole for any stragglers. It is a good idea to leave this box until dusk so that all the bees go into it. Then you can gently cover any holes, wrap the box in a cotton sheet and then drive your bees to their new hive. The bees will start to cluster, hanging from the top bars. They can be gently poured, swept or placed into your top-bar hive where they should take up residence and start building their magical comb.

Take some from an established hive

If you have a beekeeping friend you could try putting some of the top bars from your hive into his or her established hive. When comb has been built, brood laid and nurse bees are around to tend to the babies, you can transfer these top bars into your hive with a new queen.

Lemon balm – a long shot

Try rubbing the insides of your positioned hive with lemon balm herb – there is a very small chance that a passing swarm may find it and choose to stay.

Put the word out

If you want to start a new hive, let your local beekeeping club know. You can then be informed if there are any swarms in your area or if anybody wants to split their hive and has a spare nucleus of bees.

The top bars from the hive are placed over the top of the box; the bees will hang from these. By dusk all the bees will settle in the box and it can be removed to a new hive.

Buying bees

It is possible to buy a small nucleus, or 'nuc'. This generally consists of four frames of brood, honey, a queen and about 4000 bees. The problem is that these nucs come on Landstroth frames, which don't fit into a top bar. Transferring them to a top-bar hive is not easy, but it can be done with help from a friend. Cut the bottom of the wooden frame and the wire with some strong wire cutters, so that the Langstroth frame is the same shape as the internal dimensions of the top-bar hive. (One way is to lay the nuc frame on top of the follower board of the top-bar hive as a guide while cutting.) Unfortunately, some brood and comb are sacrificed. Hopefully, as top-bar hives become more popular, getting brood, honey and bees for them will become easier.

See how it's done

Watch me demonstrate how to hive a recently caught swarm of bees in a top-bar hive at:
www.youtube.com/watch?v=0N38_f89Uq0

LEGAL REQUIREMENTS

- Most councils allow you to keep a hive in an urban space; many allow two. Check with your local council regarding any particular regulations or by-laws (search on their website under *by-laws: bees*).

- You will need to register your hive with Assure Quality, which currently costs from $30 a year.

- Your hive needs to be checked for disease at least twice a year. You can do this yourself if you attend a half-day course, or get a certified beekeeper to do it for you.

- You need to complete an annual disease form for each hive.

- Hives need to be treated for varroa mite, which costs around $20 per hive each year.

It is important to be a responsible beekeeper and undertake these disease checks and treatments, as it protects all the bees in your community.

Top-bar hives comply with all New Zealand regulations under the Biosecurity (National Foulbrood Pest Management Strategy) Order 1998. This is the main legislation that beekeepers need to follow. I can personally guarantee this, as I was visited by the head of the National Foulbrood Pest Management Strategy, who came to find out about top-bar hives and, in particular, to check that they complied with the regulations. The main obligations are that:

- honeybees are kept in movable frame hives

- the hives are accessible, and

- regular checks for American Foulbrood and other exotic diseases are carried out.

If you are thinking of keeping bees in a top-bar hive, please be responsible and legal. Get your hive registered, check regularly for disease and attend an American Foulbrood disease recognition course.

See how it's done

Fine out how to treat bees organically for varroa at: www.youtube.com/watch?v=SL_qCx67VbA

Find out more

Urban backyard beekeeping is becoming very popular, as people discover how low maintenance, fascinating and rewarding keeping bees can be. If you are interested in keeping bees, I encourage you to:

- read up on the subject (borrow books from your library)

- join your local beekeeping club

- visit the website of the Save Our Bees Charitable Trust (www.saveourbees.org.nz) – this website is full of advice and support for people wanting to keep bees in a top-bar hive. You can download free plans and instructions on how to make your own top-bar hive (or a list of builders who can make one for you), plus there's a backyard beekeeping forum and information on free workshops

- register for my monthly free e-newsletter, which gives you monthly advice on what to do with your top-bar hive. Visit www.greenurbanliving.co.nz/signup.php to register.

Two ideas to steal

1 Make your own beeswax candles

You will need:

- one metre of medium-sized wick (buy at craft shops)

- beeswax: buy at craft shops, bee supply stores, or collect from your own bees

- heatproof containers for candles, e.g. shot glasses, old teacups, tin cans, paua shells, egg cups or walnut shells

Cut wicks to the length of the containers. Loop the tops of the wicks around bamboo skewers, tape in place and sit skewers over the tops of the containers. Melt the wax using a double boiler on the stovetop. Add a few drops of essential oil if you wish. When the wax is liquid, carefully pour it into the containers, making sure the wicks stay straight in the middle of the candle. Allow to cool for an hour before you remove the skewers. Trim wicks to one centimetre above the wax. Light and enjoy. Keep doors and windows closed while making your candles or you could have bees coming in to investigate what you are doing with their wax.

Checking on my bees.

2 Make your own beeswax lip balm

A great idea for Christmas gifts or to pamper yourself. Makes about one and a half cups.

You will need:

- 250 ml almond oil

- 1/2 cup grated beeswax (grate a beeswax candle)

- 3 tablespoons honey

- fresh calendula petals from four flowers

- a microwave-safe bowl

- small containers with lids (e.g. old medicine jars, skin cream pots, glass jars)

Put the almond oil and washed calendula petals in a clear glass jar and place in a sunny position for five days. This will create an oil infusion of calendula.

Strain the almond oil, then place the almond oil and beeswax in a microwave-safe bowl. Microwave on high for one minute or until the mixture melts. Whisk the honey into the mixture until thoroughly mixed. When cool but still liquid, pour into containers with lids. Apply to lips as moisturiser, or on top of lipstick for extra shine.

Use bamboo skewers (or pencils) to support the wicks as you gently pour the molten wax into the candle moulds. Allow to set for one hour before you remove the skewers and trim the wicks.

Old teacups look great as candles – they are easy to find at second-hand stores. Christmas presents sorted!

CHAPTER
NINE

USING WATER SUSTAINABLY

THE DOWNSIDE OF EDIBLE GARDENING IS THAT FOOD PLANTS ARE INHERENTLY THIRSTY IN SUMMER. WITH MANY TOWNIES EXPERIENCING HIGH WATER CHARGES, IT IS IMPORTANT TO FIND SUSTAINABLE WAYS OF USING WATER IN THE GARDEN.

Plants wrapped up warmly with a woollen blanket!

Luckily there are a number of simple, easy ways to conserve water. It makes sense to use some of the following ideas to help you save money, watering time, and a precious natural resource. Rainwater is also much better for your plants, and if you are making compost teas you will produce a much better brew if you use rainwater as opposed to the town supply, as the chemicals added to the water supply inhibit microbe activity.

MULCH

Mulching your garden with a thick layer of organic matter is one of the easiest ways to help conserve water for your plants. Not only does it stop water evaporating, but it also deters weeds and keeps the soil warm, which is good for early spring planting.

You can use all manner of materials – the best is always something you can get in large quantities for free. Good mulching materials include:

- pea straw
- straw
- sheep dags
- pine needles
- coffee grounds
- shredded newspaper, and
- leaves.

Before you apply the mulch, water the garden well. Then cover all bare soil with a mulch layer at least 10 cm deep.

Materials to avoid

Don't use hay, as it contains seedheads and you will end up with weeds throughout your garden. Avoid bark mulch and sawdust in the vegetable garden – as these materials break down they rob the soil of nitrogen. They are fine for paths and perennial beds.

IRRIGATION

BURIED CLAY POTS

This method of irrigation was invented by farmers in North Africa thousands of years ago, and is up to ten times more efficient than conventional ways of irrigating. It uses unglazed clay pots (called ollas), which are porous and allow water to seep out slowly. A combination of domestic rainwater barrels and ollas could provide all your garden irrigation needs in a green urban garden. This method is also cheaper and more reliable than many drip or spray irrigation systems, which often clog or break.

The pot needs to be unglazed and able to hold between two and five litres. Ideally it should have a bulbous base and a thin neck. I have been unable to find anything like that, so I use terracotta pots from the garden centre. If the pot comes with a drainage hole, use a cork to bung it up. It also needs a fitted lid to prevent mosquitoes breeding in it. I use an old bread and butter plate or a pot saucer.

I always grow my lettuce around an olla pot. This stops them becoming bitter through lack of water. I use unglazed terracotta pots from the garden centre.

To install an olla, dig a hole three times as wide and twice as deep as the pot. If you have heavy clay soil, mix in some compost and sand. Set the pot in place with the rim about two centimetres above the surface. Firm the soil around the pot, fill it with water and put on the lid. In most soil, your plants need to be within five centimetres of the pot. Check the pots often. In hot weather, smaller ones will need filling every two to three days.

Water is drawn out of the pot by the roots of the plants. I add 'worm wees' (see page 123) or a compost tea brew (see page 116) to the pots if plants need a boost.

This is a particularly good way of irrigating lettuce in summer – lettuce becomes bitter if it does not have a constant water supply.

See how it's done

Watch me demonstrate how to set up an olla in a vegetable garden at:
http://www.youtube.com/watch?v=lOVfnppdn28

LEAKY HOSES

These hoses are porous membranes made out of recycled vehicle tyres. You can buy rolls of them at garden centres and home hardware stores. They are cheap and easy to install. Bury leaky hoses under the mulch layer. Watering the root zone rather than the leaves in this way helps prevent summer fungal disease on many vegetables.

A leaky hose made from recycled rubber. Bury under the mulch layer to irrigate the root zone of your plants.

SWALES

A swale is a shallow trench dug along the contour line. Rainwater run-off is slowed and collected in these trenches, making it available for the plants to use. This is a very simple system, and it works particularly well if your garden is on a slope. My vegetable garden is positioned on a sloping terrace, so I plant rows of plants along the contour and form shallow trenches on the upper side to collect rainwater.

A swale is a very simple but effective technique for trapping water and making it available for your plants.

HOMEMADE DRIP IRRIGATION

If you have an old hose that has split or is always kinking, don't throw it away – reuse it for irrigation. Use a cordless drill to make tiny holes in the last metre of its length. Install a screw-on cap at the end and you have an instant, low-tech drip irrigation system. Bury it under the mulch and attach it to your tap or water barrel.

The roots of this young apple tree are absorbing water being slowly released from two large containers. Position containers around the drip zones of trees. Mulch underneath trees to stop grass and weeds from growing.

ONE DROP AT A TIME

Make individual plant waterers by drilling a small hole in buckets, milk bottles or any other larger plastic containers, filling them with water and placing around trees or thirsty plants. These containers release water slowly. Fill from the hose whenever you are passing. You can also add compost tea to the water mixture to feed new trees and shrubs (see page 123).

WINE BAG WATERER

The wine bladders that come in cask wine make great little waterers. Cut off the corner of the bag opposite the spigot, fill the bag with water and then secure with a rubber band or hair tie. Place the spigot face down on the soil and adjust the spigot so that it very slowly drips. (If the bag has a push-button spigot, wedge a small stick or toothpick into the button to keep it open.) Use an old leaking hot-water bottle for the same job.

Being a woman I can multi-task – gardening is thirsty work and there is a lot of fine Hawke's Bay wine to be sampled!

WATERING TIPS

- Always water at dusk (or dawn if you're an early bird), not in the middle of a hot day. Plants are better adapted to take up water at dawn and dusk, and less water is lost to evaporation.

- Water with a hand-held hose rather than automatic irrigation; this prevents overwatering, and you can direct water where it is required. (Manually watering your garden can be a very relaxing pastime, especially if you have a glass of wine in the other hand.)

- Water less often but deeply. This encourages strong root systems to grow deep into the soil rather than along the surface.

- Always remove some of the mulch layer to check moisture levels. Often the mulch feels dry when the soil underneath is damp. You may find you don't need to water.

- Reduce the size of your lawn – they are thirsty monsters, and you can't eat them!

- In an ornamental garden, consider xeriscaping. This is landscaping using drought-tolerant plants – those that have adapted to dry, hot areas such as the Mediterranean. They often have silver, spiky or waxy leaves.

INSTALL A WATER BARREL: A STEP-BY-STEP GUIDE

With droughts and hose bans becoming more common, it makes good sense to collect rainwater. In most urban situations, rainwater is washed away with all our sewerage.

It's easy to set up your own rainwater collecting system and start 'growing your own water'. You can buy water barrels from many plumbing and hardware stores, or make your own out of any container that can hold water. I use old oak wine barrels or large recycled plastic barrels. You can

A very simple and cheap rain barrel can be made out of a recycled plastic drum and some PVC piping.

also try linking several barrels. Obviously the larger the container, the greater your capacity in times of dry weather. The container requires a lid to keep out debris and mosquito larvae.

If you want to install a rainwater tank, check your local council regulations.

Step 1: Materials and tools

You will need:

- 1 food-grade plastic drum or similar
- 1 brass water tap
- plumber's tape
- downspout diverter
- concrete blocks or similar, to raise barrel at least 30 cm off the ground (the higher you can get your water barrel the more water pressure you create)
- small piece of hose as an overflow device, if your downspout diverter does not include this in its design (length can be cut to suit)

These simple tools are all that's required to install a rainwater barrel.

Tools

- permanent marker
- drill
- jigsaw or hole saw.

Step 2: Prepare and locate your barrel

Ensure the barrel is clean, and decide where to locate it. The best position is next to a downpipe that drains the main roof area, and above or near your vegetable garden. Place the concrete blocks in position and put the barrel on top, ensuring it is sitting level and securely.

Step 3: Drill holes

Mark the positions for the tap hole and the overflow (if your downpipe diverter doesn't have one) on the barrel. The tap hole should be five centimetres above the bottom of the barrel; the overflow hole should be three centimetres from the top of the barrel, directed away from the house and foundations.

Drill the tap hole to fit the diameter of the brass water tap. Wrap plumber's tape around the tap and screw it into the bottom hole.

Drill the hole for the overflow to fit the diameter of the piece of hose. Insert the hose into the drilled hole so that water overflows into the garden. You can make it as long as you need.

Trace a hole for your downpipe diverter on top of the barrel. Cut out with the jigsaw. Following the manufacturer's instructions, fit the downpipe diverter so that rainwater will flow into the barrel.

Step 4: Wait for rain!

I fitted an old-fashioned hand pump to the top of our rain barrel. The kids love playing with it – a great optional extra.

New Zealand suppliers of rainwater diverters:

www.ecodrain.co.nz

www.hedgehog.cc

I fitted an old-fashioned hand pump to the top of our rain barrel. The kids love playing with it – a great optional extra.

GROWING WATER CROPS

Water crops are an efficient way to grow food in what is often a forgotten space. If you have a boggy area or pond in your garden, consider growing some of these.

By definition, water crops require damp or swampy conditions throughout their growing season. As you will be eating these crops, it is imperative that you use clean water, so grow them near an outside tap, or divert rainwater from the roof into large pots, half barrels, old bathtubs or troughs.

Chinese water chestnuts

These chestnuts have a sweet nutty flavour with a crunchy texture. You peel them, then eat raw or cook and add to stir-fries and salads.

The plant (its scientific name is *Eleocharis dulcis*) grows from spreading rhizomes. They like a warm sunny spot with rich soil about 30 cm deep. I add some animal manure to the compost for an extra boost. Plant the corms 30 cm apart and 4 cm deep with the growing tips pointing up. Keep moist, and add water as the plants grow. They need to be flooded in at least 10 cm of water during the summer.

If mosquito larvae become a problem, pour half a cup of vegetable oil onto the surface of the water. The oil will suffocate the larvae but won't hurt the plant. (Use your cheapest cooking oil, not your finest extra virgin!)

These plants require at least six months of frost-free weather to develop. When the tops start to die off in early winter they are ready to be harvested. Drain the water (if growing in a pot) and sort through the soil for the corms. In a good season a single corm can multiply to over 50. Cut off the tops. You can store the corms in the fridge, or blanch and freeze. Save some to plant next spring.

Buy fresh corms to grow from Chinese markets, herb nurseries or online auction sites.

Water chestnuts are easy to grow. If you don't have a pond, use any large deep pot or container – a plastic tub lined with plastic rubbish bags will do. To harvest, turn the pot upside down and rummage through the wet soil for the corms. Keep the container flooded with water during hot summer weather. The chestnuts are ready to harvest once the green stalks start to die off in early winter.

Watercress

Watercress is brimming with healthy vitamins and minerals. If you enjoy eating watercress, grow it rather than collecting it from streams – wild watercress can be contaminated by a liver fluke, so is best avoided.

Contrary to what many people think, this plant does not have to be grown in running water, but it does need wet feet at all times. If you have a boggy area in your garden, try growing it there. If you don't, any container without drainage holes can be used to successfully grow watercress. (I grow mine in polystyrene tubs, which you can

pick up for a few dollars from fish markets.) Make four holes around the side of the tub, halfway up. This creates constantly wet soil. Fill with potting mix then plant the seeds, or if you have some fresh watercress, try planting some of the stems. The plant is usually easily grown from cuttings. Keep the soil moist. Watercress likes some shade in the heat of summer.

Recycle polystyrene tubs to grow watercress.

To harvest, simply cut the leaves just above ground level. Leave the roots to re-sprout. Enjoy in sandwiches, stews, soups and salads.

Regular harvesting of watercress tips prevents it bolting to seed in summer. Use scissors to cut the tender tips.

You can buy watercress seeds from kingsseeds.co.nz, or fresh plants from farmers' markets and Chinese supermarkets.

CHAPTER TEN

GARDENING WITH KIDS

IN THIS TECHNOLOGY AGE IT'S A MISSION TO GET THE KIDS AWAY FROM THE TV OR COMPUTER AND INTO THE GARDEN – BUT IT IS WELL WORTH THE EFFORT. ONE OF THE REASONS I BECAME SO INVOLVED WITH GARDENING WAS THROUGH BEING AT HOME WITH YOUNG CHILDREN, AND WANTING THEM TO BE OUTSIDE EXPERIENCING THE NATURAL WORLD. GREEN URBAN LIVING IS NOT JUST ABOUT GROWING FOOD, IT'S ALSO ABOUT INVOLVING THE KIDS AND GETTING THEM TO RECONNECT WITH NATURE.

A snack track is a healthy alternative to other after-school snacks.

My children take it for granted that they can free range after dinner, munching on snow peas and freshly pulled carrots, or wrangling an escaped chicken. They don't know how lucky they are. They are having the childhood I had, roaming around the neighbourhood with friends, climbing trees, chasing butterflies, picking flowers and enjoying all manner of pets.

No matter how small your backyard is, you can provide some of these experiences for your children.

The secret to gardening with kids is to make it fun and exciting, and to involve all the senses, especially taste, touch and smell. Don't wrap your kids in bubble wrap. Let them explore, get dirty, climb trees, eat carrots with dirt on them and cuddle their chooks. Children don't notice a professionally landscaped garden or views. They are interested in what is right in front of their noses: what it tastes like, how it smells, and what they can use it for. To avoid clashes between neat formal gardens and rampaging kids, give some space over to the children. An area dedicated to growing food and flowers, supporting all manner of creepy crawlies and birdlife, and full of nooks and crannies, may not be orderly and calm, but provides a wonderful, safe and evolving place of discovery for your children.

Try growing an 'after-school snack track'. Form a small circular path and grow strawberries, lemonade citrus, cocktail kiwifruit, raspberries, baby carrots, snow peas, mandarins, cherry tomatoes and beans. When the kids come home from school, send them out to the garden to forage. Once they get used to munching these foods straight from the garden, they'll think nothing of grazing on asparagus, broad beans and broccoli plucked fresh off the plant.

MAKE A WILLOW WIGWAM: A STEP-BY-STEP GUIDE

This is a great project to do with the kids over winter when not much is happening in the garden. It ticks all the 'gurbing' boxes, as it's fun, easy, quick and free. You need to harvest the willow in winter when the tree is dormant.

Step 1: Cut some willow branches

Go down to your local river or lake edge and collect some long lengths of living willow branches. They need to be two to three centimetres thick.

Step 2: Design your wigwam

Decide where you want to build the wigwam – somewhere that receives some sun but is not too dry in summer is ideal. Using a hose or string line, lay the outline of your design on the ground. Get artistic and design entry and exit tunnels or archways, and make it to a child's scale so no adult can gain entry.

Step 3: Build your wigwam

Push the willow branches into the soil to a depth of at least 10 cm. Keep the branches close together so that when they grow, they form a dense interwoven wall. A roof can be formed by bending over the tops of the willow and securing with string.

Make a willow tunnel. This sort of space provides a cool place to play in summer. Try making a willow arch as an entranceway to a hut or playhouse.

Come spring the branches will burst into life and form a thick, woven green wall. Keep it well watered during the hotter months.

Step 4: Wigwam maintenance

Keep the wigwam watered over spring and summer and your kids will have a living hut to play in. In summer I grow snow peas, sweet peas and runner beans up the outside for my kids to snack on.

As the willow grows and branches, weave the side branches through the uprights to form a thick wall. You could cut or form a window as the willow grows.

Snow peas are great to grow in a kids' garden, as they are fast to grow and sweet to eat.

This sort of space provides a cool place to play in summer. Try making a willow arch as an entranceway to a hut or playhourse.

Grow vegetables that kids can pop straight into their mouths.

Make a scarecrow with the kids. Give him a name and personlity, and plant him in your garden.

An old car tyre from a tyre shop makes a strong and robust swing. It won't cost you a cent and will last for years.

HOW TO GROW AND MAKE BIRDHOUSE GOURDS

Growing gourds and using them to make birdhouses is a great outdoor project to do with the kids. The gourds grow during summer, cure in autumn and are ready to make into birdhouses in winter. They provide an inside activity for kids when it's wet and cold outside.

Gourds come from the same family as pumpkins and squashes. Most are inedible. You can buy seeds at most garden centres.

PLANTING THE SEEDS

These plants are easy to grow. Remember all those pumpkin seedlings that germinate in your worm farm or compost? Gourds, being closely related, are just as easy.

Plant three seeds in a large pot and plant out the strongest one when established. Birdhouse gourds

Scoffing freshly shelled peas is an easy way of ensuring your kids are getting their five plus a day.

like well-drained, enriched soil. As it grows it will trail along the ground, so it will need some space.

You can get clever and try growing strange-shaped gourds: place the plant in a small wooden frame – as the gourd grows it will take on this internal shape!

HARVESTING THE GOURDS

Gourds are ready to be harvested when the stalk becomes dry in late autumn. Cut each gourd with at least five centimetres of stalk attached. Handle carefully as they bruise easily at this stage. Wipe off any moisture and keep them in a cool and airy place to dry for around three months. Make sure the gourds are not touching each other to allow for plenty of air circulation. If mould appears, just wipe it off with a damp cloth soaked in bleach. If any of the gourds start to rot, toss them into the compost pile or worm farm.

MAKING THE BIRDHOUSE

As the gourds dry they change colour, and each takes on its own particular hew of brown. Gourds that are fully dried will be lightweight, and will rattle when shaken hard. Small ones cure quickly, and large ones can take up to six months.

- Rub gourd with a medium-grade sandpaper. Wear a dust mask, as any mould may be toxic.

- Using a small hole-saw or spade bit, drill a three-to-five-centimetre hole in the middle of the gourd to provide a front door for the bird.

- Under this entry hole, drill a small hole in which to fit a piece of branch or bamboo as a perch. You could thread the perch right through the gourd and out a small exit hole to make it really stable. Anchor with a small spot of glue if necessary. (Experiment with entrance hole sizes for the birds found in your locality. From experience it seems best to go too small rather than too large.)

A gourd flower and developing gourd. As the gourd grows you can etch patterns or names into the outside skin, or place in a wooden box to grow your own unique masterpieces.

Dry the freshly picked gourds in the sun for a few days and then move into a sheltered place to fully dry and cure. This can take up to six months for the largest ones.

- Drill a few small holes on the underside of the gourd for drainage, as well as two holes on either side at the very top of the neck. Those last two holes are for threading a wire through so that you can hang the birdhouse outside.

- Remove all seeds and pulp from inside the gourd. If you have trouble reaching it all, put some small stones or gravel inside and shake to release the rest of the seeds and pulp.

- Optional: paint, stain or varnish the outside of the gourd before you hang it, to make it last longer.

Paint or stain the gourd, or use exterior varnish if you prefer the more natural look.

Equipment required to make your birdhouses includes some sandpaper, a cordless drill, a spade bit and some varnish or stain.

Rub the gourd with sandpaper to smooth and remove any mould.

Some new real estate for the local bird population! Hang the finished gourds high in a tree away from prowling cats and protected from the wind.

MAKE SOME SEED BOMBS

Seed bombs are randomly thrown by guerrilla gardeners in large urban cities, such as New York, to revegetate unused vacant lots and neglected public spaces. Why not do a spot of guerrilla gardening in your backyard? Kids love to throw these balls around the place and watch the plants develop.

Seed bombs are hard clay balls with seeds inside. They need to be thrown onto bare soil, where they will absorb moisture from the ground, as well as dew and rain. They will sprout when conditions are right. In the meantime the clay protects the seeds from animals and the wind.

Many seeds can sprout from a single bomb, but they will fight it out for world (garden) domination.

Seed bomb recipe

- 5 parts red terracotta clay (buy from craft shop)

- 3 parts homemade compost: this must be your very best vintage, with lots of natural microbes. You should be able to see white fungi threads throughout the mixture.

- 1 part used coffee grounds

- 1 part seeds of your choice. You could use a wildflower mix, herb seeds, beneficial plant mix, sunflowers, poppies, or anything else that takes the kids' fancy.

Mix all the ingredients together without adding water (unless the clay is very dry). You will have to knead it like dough to get all the materials incorporated. Roll into small round balls, about the size of a large marble. Dry for two days in the sun. When totally dry they will change from a dark clay colour to a light brown colour, and will be rock hard. Store in a dry, cool place until required. Get the kids out with their slingshots or cricket throwing arms, and scatter the bombs around.

The finished product. After drying it will be ready to be hurled around the garden!

When dry, the seed bombs change to a light colour and are rock hard.

Encourage some 'good guy' insects by building a Bug Hilton with your kids.

MAKE YOUR OWN SEED TAPES

This is a great project to do with the kids in spring, to kick-start the growing action in the garden. Seed tapes are lengths of biodegradable paper with seeds incorporated into them at set distances. The idea is to lay the tape flat on top of the soil, cover with a fine layer of soil and let nature take its course. This method avoids oversowing or having to transplant seedlings into the garden, and you end up with neat straight lines of vegetables (great for the Virgos amongst us!). The tapes are also easy for little hands to handle. This method particularly suits small seeds such as carrots, lettuce, onions, spring onions, leeks, mesclun and basil.

You can make your own seed tapes using toilet tissue, flour and water and a pastry brush. Plant them in the garden or give away to friends.

Seed tape recipe

You will need:

- a thick paste made from flour and water

- a small brush (a pastry or art brush is perfect)

- a length of toilet tissue (about 30 cm is a good length for little hands)

- seeds to sow

Lie a section of toilet tissue on a flat surface. Paint flour paste thickly down middle of the length with brush. Sprinkle seeds very thinly into the paste, allowing for around 8–10 cm spacings between seeds. Cover with another length of toilet tissue and pat down gently. Lie tissue flat under a weight, such as stacked books, until dry. Lay flat in the garden and cover with a fine, thin layer of soil. Water with fine spray and keep moist until germination.

It's best not to plant seed tapes on a windy day – the seed tapes will quickly become flags.

MAKE A BUG HILTON

My three young boys love nothing better than hunting for creepy crawlies to proudly show their mother, or to feed to a lucky chicken.

Insects play an incredibly important role in any organic garden, and by providing the right sort of habitat you can hopefully attract them as

Harvest edible flowers from areas where you know they will be spray free.

long-term tenants. Beneficial insects include ladybirds, lacewings, damselflies, wasps, hoverflies and bees. Unfortunately, like many organisms, beneficial insects are under threat from pesticides, spreading suburbia and agriculture. Providing a

secure haven in your garden allows these good guys an excuse to make it their permanent home.

These sorts of insects seem to prefer individual tunnels to either lay eggs or hibernate in during the winter months. A 'Bug Hilton' is a structure full of lots of different-sized nooks and crannies that should fit the bill. Remember, you also need to provide a food source of flowers, shrubs and pests.

I like to think of a Bug Hilton as garden art with a purpose. It can be made out of any recycled material, including bamboo, timber, straw, branches and tiles. An ideal apartment should be at least 15 cm in diameter and about 50 cm off the ground.

I made mine out of a wooden pallet, which I cut into sections with a handsaw and then stacked. After a beach- and forest-combing session with the kids, we filled the spaces with shells, bunches of twigs, pine cones, bamboo canes, large seed pods, blocks of firewood, and pumice with holes drilled in it (I drilled these holes with a slight incline to avoid them filling with rainwater). Studies have found that most of the beneficial insects prefer holes of a certain diameter. The most preferred tunnel sizes seem to be 4 mm or 9 mm in diameter, and 8–10 mm deep.

Place your Bug Hilton in a sunny spot protected from wind, and wait for all those good guys to take up residence.

Many people ask me how I keep the cockroaches and white-tailed spiders out, but the truth is you can't. But even these mini-beasts have some benefit in the garden, if not in the house!

Even if you don't do much in the way of gardening, there should be room for at least one beneficial insect apartment in your garden. They take up hardly any space, and are a great family project to enjoy with the kids, not to mention a conversation starter with adult visitors.

See how it's done

Watch Liam explain how we made our Bug Hilton at:
http://www.youtube.com/watch?v=oMKjgHnezok

MAKE LOLLY FLOWERS

Making these sweet treats is easy and fun. Use only edible flowers that haven't been sprayed with insecticide or pesticide (including homemade sprays). Suitable flowers include: rose (petals), violets, borage, calendula, nasturtium, elderflowers, dandelions, sage, rosemary, rocket, apple blossom and cornflowers.

Instructions

- Wash freshly picked flowers with fresh water.

- Beat an egg white until it is stiff and forms peaks.

- Paint the egg white foam all over the flower, using an artist's brush or pastry brush.

- Using a small sieve, lightly dust the flowers with caster or icing sugar.

- Gently lay the flowers on a sheet of waxed paper, and place in sun until the flowers feel stiff when touched.

- Use straight away – let the kids enjoy as is, or use to decorate cup cakes, smoothies or any other sweet delights.

FURTHER READING

PERMACULTURE

Creative Sustainable Gardening in New Zealand for the Twenty-first Century
by Diana Anthony, David Bateman.

Design Your Own Orchard: Bringing Permaculture Design to the Ground in Aotearoa
by Kay Baxter, Body and Soul Publishing.

Food Not Lawns: How to Turn Your Yard into a Garden and Your Neighbourhood into a Community
by H.C. Flores, Chelsea Green Publishing Company.

Paradise In Your Garden
by Jenny Allen, New Holland Publishers (AUS) Ltd.

Permaculture: A Designer's Manual
by Bill Mollison, Tagari Publications.

The Permaculture: Home Garden
by Linda Woodrow, Penguin Group.

GROWING FRUIT AND VEGETABLES

Fresh Food From Small Spaces: The Square Inch Gardener's Guide to Year-round Growing, Fermenting, and Sprouting
by R.J. Ruppenthal, Chelsea Green Publishing Company.

Gardening in New Zealand Month by Month
by Dennis Greville, New Holland Publishers (NZ) Ltd.

Garden Wisdom and Know-How: Everything You Need to Know to Plant, Grow and Harvest
by the editors of Rodale Gardening Books, Black Dog and Leventhal Publishing.

Get Fresh
by Dennis Greville, New Holland Publishers (NZ) Ltd.

Growing Organic
by Phillipa Jamieson and Nick Hamilton, New Holland Publishers (NZ) Ltd.

'Grow Your Own Fresh, Healthy Fruit from Homegrown Fruit Trees', *NZ Gardener*, 2009, Fairfax Publishing.

Home Fruit Growing in New Zealand
by Dale Williams, Government Printer.

Koanga Garden Guide: A Complete Guide to Gardening Organically and Sustainably
by Kay Baxter, Body and Soul Publishing.

Organic: Don Burkes's Guide to Growing Organic Food
by Don Burke, New Holland Publishers (Aus) Ltd.

Self-sufficency: Herbs and spices
by Linda Gray, New Holland Publishers (UK) Ltd.

The Best of Jackie French: A Practical Guide to Everything from Aphids to Zucchini Chocolate Cake
by Jackie French, HarperCollins Publishing.

The Wilderness Garden
by Jackie French, Arid Books.

COMPOSTING

Let it Rot! The Home Gardener's Guide to Composting
by Stu Cambell, Garden Way Publishing, USA.

CHICKENS

Backyard Poultry, Naturally
by Alanna Moore, Bolwarrah Press.

Keep Chickens! Tending Small Flocks in Cities, Suburbs and Other Small Places
by Barbara Kilarski, Storey Publishing.

Self-sufficiency: Hen Keeping
by Michael Hatcher, New Holland Publishers (UK) Ltd.

BEES

Elimination of American Foulbrood Disease without the Use of Drugs, A practical Manual for Beekeepers
by Mark Goodwin, National Beekeepers' Association of New Zealand (Inc).

First Lessons in Beekeeping
by Keith Delaplane, Dadant & Sons.

Self-sufficiency: Beekeeping
by Joanna Ryde, New Holland Publishers (UK) Ltd.

The Barefoot Beekeeper: A Simple, Sustainable Approach to Small-scale Beekeeping Using Top bar Hives
by P.J. Chandler, www.biobees.com

SELF-SUFFICIENCY

Eco-Kids Self-sufficiency Handbook
by Alan and Gill Bridgewater, New Holland Publishers (NZ) Ltd.

Living Green
by Annmaree Kane and Christina Neubert, New Holland Publishers (NZ) Ltd.

Mastering the Art of Self-sufficiency in New Zealand
by Carolann Murray, New Holland Publishers (NZ) Ltd.

The Good Life
by Francesca Price, New Holland Publishers (NZ) Ltd.

The publishers would also like to recommend the following books from the Self-sufficiency series available from New Holland Publishers (NZ) Ltd:

Cheesemaking, Foraging, Grow your Own Fruit and Vegetables, Home Brewing, Household Cleaning, Preserving, Soap Making and Spinning, Dyeing and Weaving.

INDEX